THE SCARS THAT HEALED

To: My brother Peter E.

ERIC E.J. JONES

Copyright © 2022 by Eric E.J. Jones

ISBN: 978-1-64810-198-4

All rights reserved. No part of this book may be reproduced mechanically, electronically, virtually, or by any other means, including photocopying without written permission of the publisher. It is illegal to copy this book, post it to any website or distribute it by any other means without permission from the publisher.

Published by Perfect Publishing Co.

ACKNOWLEDGEMENT

I extend a special thanks to my friends whom I look to as my brothers, Paul Morrison, Rene Martinez, Tony Felder, Greg Felder, Darrell Young, Frank Burgo, Jeff Burgo, Demetra Moore, Keith Brown, Andre Peeples, Dujuan Stubbs, Stephen Gousby, Rodney Lawson. To my childhood friends Brian Edge, Willie (June) Stallworth, Eric (Sam) Stallworth (R.I.P.), Michael Robinson, Armon Irons, Terry Lowery, Ricky Blackman, David Alvarez, Tyrone Gulley, Damian Prather, Andrew St. Aime., Delon White, Richard Ash, Chris Vaughn, Ron Lopes, Daryl Simmons, Dennis Franklin, Elmer Bruce and Jay White. Thank you all for being a part of my life journey and allowing me to be a part of yours.

PREFACE

Growing up in Mattapan, Massachusetts as a kid I never knew how many twists and turns livinglife in the inner-city would have on me. Coming up in an era where many things were not discussed in my home such as drugs, gangs, prostitution, and sex left me with no other alternative but to become street smart and also my own teacher. Life for the most part, in the beginning, seemed easy just obey the rules of your parents and make it home before the street lights come on and whatever was prepared for dinner you ate or ate nothing at all.

Although these golden rules were instilled in me, at times I'd be forced into situations where I would have to break them. Some of life's faced situations would warrant me to stand my groundand create my own set of rules that only I would follow. Many encounters throughout life forcedme to grow up faster than I would have wanted to and skip right from childhood to adulthood without any knowledge about advancing to the next stage of life.

Being raised in an environment within the inner-city where the life expectancy of a black man was the age of 21 trying to defeat those odds would be quite challenging. Navigating through thecity of Boston where gang violence was at an all time high, drugs being used and sold on every corner and shootings happening randomly, often had me wondering if I'd live one day to the next.

Let me take you on a journey about my life where some of the situations faced would cause me to make life-changing decisions. In many situations throughout this story, there were many timeswhen I knew I was in the wrong but had to make a bad choice. In other instances, some bad karma came my way which had me ultimately questioning my purpose here on earth. The reality of trauma and what it felt and looked like was full-blown throughout my life and the most

difficult part was not knowing how to deal with it.

Take a deep breath and prepare for a story that will send you on a roller coaster ride of differentemotions. Fasten your seatbelt and let's take a ride, just don't forget to look both ways because tragedy can strike at any moment without giving you forewarning.

LETTER TO JOSH

To my fallen comrade, Josh a.k.a. Jacked Diesel the 5-star general. Thank you for believing in me to D.J. on your show Bomb Squad Mondays on the Urban Heat. Without you even knowing it you were creating, a situation that lead up to this book. Having Mel EB as the co-host on the show led to me sharing a brief life story with both you and her. Mel in turn suggested that I write a book and had the connections in place to help me achieve the goal.

Through you connecting me with Mel I was able to meet my graphic designer James Scales and my publicist Ken Rochon. Between Mel, James, and Ken they are a powerhouse to be reckoned with and I sincerely thank you Josh for making it all happen.

Your vision and insight on things will never go missing. You were an innovator, and motivator but more importantly a childhood friend from Mattapan with whom I have a great deal of respect. The presence you displayed in a room was a look of all business and placing your best foot forward to get to the finish line. We shared plenty of different ideas and I took your insight on it all seriously.

One thing you always taught me is that you never know who is watching or listening so, your creative side always has to remain on point. I'll continue to reflect on all the jewels you dropped on me and "Smash the like Button" while doing so.

Continue to rest easy in heaven my friend, Love you

ACKNOWLEDGMENTS

I would like to thank the woman whose love never faded for me once and who always knew and understood me better than anyone else-my sister Angela! Always there to provide words of peaceand guidance no matter how troubling things may have seemed. You always gave me the reason to keep on believing and achieving even at times when I felt hopeless.

Although we shared some of the same hurdles in life it was the energy and positive vibes from you that continued to feed my soul. Anytime I needed a shoulder to lean on yours was rock solid to give me the ongoing support I needed. You were always referred to as being my twin and eventhough we were a little shy of two years apart I can see why many people thought so due to the similarities in our facial features. There honestly wasn't anything on this earth I would not do foryou.

I'd like to also thank a host of family and friends who continued to believe in me and always hadmy back when it counted the most. My heartfelt appreciation goes out to aunts Elaine, Priscilla, and Kathleen for being the ear to listen when I needed someone to talk to. To my Uncle's Dewayne, Robert and Claude thank you for always filling me up with words of visdom to help navigate through the processes of life.

I extend a special thanks to my friends whom I look to ʽny brothers, Paul Morrison, Rene Martinez, Tony Felder, G. Felder, Darrell Young, Frank Burgo, Jeff Burgo, Demetra Mo\, Keith Brown, Andre Peeples, Dujuan Stubbs, Stephen Gous. Rodney Lawson. To my childhood friends Brian Edge, ʽllie (June) Stallworth, Eric (Sam) Stallworth (R.I.P.),

Michael Robinson, Armon Irons, Terry Lowery, Ricky Blackman, David Alvarez, Tyrone Gulley, Damian Prather, Andrew St. Aime., Delon White, Richard Ash, Chris Vaughn, Daryl Simmons, Dennis Franklin, Elmer Bruce and Jay White. Thank you all for being a part of my life journey and allowing me to be a part of yours.

Finally, I would like to acknowledge my children Alyssa, Eric, and Tevin for being my "REASON" and the "WHY" I keep on going.

MEL EB'S NOTE TO THE AUTHOR:

The first time I shared the same studio space with Eric Jones I'll admit I was bowled over by his stature. Admittingly at first, I was expecting Eric to have a booming voice that overpowered the room. The truth is that Eric's very calm monotone voice was a pleasant surprise. Our mutual friend Jack Diesel "The 5-Star General" was the great mastermind that brought both Eric and I together. Jack Diesel was an innovator way before his time- it honestly was not a surprise that "J" believed that both Eric and I belonged together in the studio. Within a few Mondays togetherin the radio studio it was clear the writing was on the wall that our team had that special spark and Jack Diesel's brilliant foresight was going to pay off. I approach each show knowing that I must bring my "A-Game" being Eric must and will be running full-throttle expecting me to meet him toe-for-toe in wit and charm on-air. Our synergy on-air is felt by all that hear our voices overthe airwaves.

One of the greatest lessons I have learned from Eric is past transgressions are not a predictor ofwhere you are going to land in our personal lives. The human spirit is such a marvelous instrument that if it is used correctly, it can and will become a sword and not a stumbling block. Perseverance can only be found in the souls of people that have found their rock-bottom and their why-as to what and why they are pushing themselves to greatness. My personal experiences have been rooted in human predictability. A great example of this is individuals willtalk a "good-game". You will hear, "I'm going to" -" I plan to start" - "I'm going to let you know". Eric has completely taken this thought process of mine and flipped it on its head. I watched the determination of a man focused not only on the goal, but his vision. He took the ideaand hope of writing this book to a measurable accomplishment. Eric has a surgical way of negotiating complex personal relationships that have been impacted by the inner-city street's politics. People respond to Eric's words and presence with respect. Like a well-loved Boston Politician Eric can move through a crowded room being greeted with hugs, smiles, and daps from the homies. Man and woman respond to Eric all in the same way with smiles of familiarity from years of friendship and mutual respect.

The book The Scares That Healed is packed with powerful teachable human experiences. I foundmyself at times wanting to jump into the pages of the book to defend and protect both Eric and his sister. The relatable descriptions given in this book not only created a compelling plea of the injustices felt by a social system and society that failed Eric on many levels. The pages of coming-up on the urban inner-streets of Boston that claimed the lives of black men from our community for decades. Eric's persuasive bird's eye view of his personal perception of the black male's life in just another America's nameless urban hoods- the belly of beast.

THE SCARS THAT HEALED

In February of 1970, my sister Angela was born in Mocksville, North Carolina. Our parents were both born in raised in Salisbury, North Carolina. Both of them migrated to Boston, Massachusetts to search for better working careers as at the time the rate of pay was better in the north than that of the south. On December 18, 1971, I was born my mom gave birth to me at Boston City Hospital not sure how much I weighed or what time I was born. My parents both worked my father at the meat market and my mom at a bank in Boston. Years later my dad started working for a manufacturing company. In the early 70s, we lived in a couple of apartments before my mom and dad purchased their first home in Mattapan on Hollingsworth Street. Growing up on my street at the time it was a predominately white neighborhood and not many blacks lived on my street. As a kid, it was a great experience because it gave me and my sister the opportunity to play with and become friends with other kids in the neighborhood who came from different backgrounds. I and my sister Angela did a lot together and although we were 1 year apart, we were joined at the hip as if we were twins. Many folks often thought we were twins because we looked so much alike. Our facial features were the same and complexion as well. Starting out in the school system my parents had us placed into the Metco school program my sister attended school in Weston and me in Belmont. The bus ride was so far and at the time they had what was called host families just in case a severe storm came about and I or my sister could not make it back home we'd be assigned to a family of one of our classmates as shelter until the storm passed. At the time I felt like this was a brilliant idea seeing my parents would have to travel so far to get to my sister and me and also run the risk of getting into an accident along the way.

While attending the Metco school program I was in the first grade and my sister had already been in the Metco program for about 3 years or so. Angela was two grades ahead of me but we always remained so close as kids growing up. At the ages of 5 and 7, our parents put us on our

first flight alone back then you could do that as there weren't as many violent and terrorist acts as there are today. My sister and I would fly Eastern Airlines to North Carolina for the Summer and enjoyed the flight experience by having the captain give us both a set of wings as our souvenirs

from the flight. In the Summer of 1979, my mom and dad decided to pull my sister and me out of the Metco school system and placed us in the Boston Public school system. Although the school was closer to our home the environment was very different as there were more blacks in the school than there were whites which is what we just left. We both attended the James J. Chittick School and although we did miss the Metco program it felt good to attend school with kids from our neighborhood. Many of the kids from our streets Hollingsworth, Rosewood, Rockdale, Caton, Rector, and River Street all attended the school. We would walk to school in packs sometimes there would be like 15 to 20 of us walking at the same time. Looking at us from a distance you would think we were like a marching band because there were so many of us. The only part I hated about walking to school was walking underneath that pissy tunnel at the end of my street. It was a dark tunnel that reeked of urine and at night walking through there you'd be lucky if you made it from one side to the next without getting robbed or jumped. In my mind, I'm saying to myself that and my sister went from attending school in a beautiful suburban area to now attending school in the inner city. Despite the situation, we made the best of it, and the most important part was that I and my sister now attended school together versus being apart. I knew at some point my sister would be leaving the Chittick School since it only went up to the 5th grade.

The time had come when I was in the 3rd grade and my sister in the 5th, I knew the school year would fly bad and it did. My sister graduated and was getting ready to head off to Middle School. After my sister graduated, we went down south to visit with our family which seemed to be the Summer ritual if we were not enrolled in camp. The Summers in North Carolina would be extremely hot air conditioners in homes were not a common thing back then.both of our grandmothers would be in their rocking chairs rocking back and forth as if the heat did not phase them at all. Visiting the south in the Summer felt like going to work. My mother's mom Sarah would have me and my sister picking corn, apples, tomatoes you name it. Our father's mother Clara didn't have us doing many outdoor chores we stayed in the house with her or just played in the yard My sister and I couldn't wait to get back home where we had A/C in the living room. We would typically head back home around the 3 rd week of August to go school shopping and pick up school supplies and other items to prepare for the school year. My sister went off to the Frank V. Thompson Middle School and I continued on at the James J. Chittick School. Starting the school year wasn't as bad as I thought it would be, I would walk to school with my childhood friends from my street June, Michael, Terry,and Armon. We had such a great brotherhood and our street was the village that raised us all of our mothers and fathers knew each other so it would be hard for us to get away with anything. 4th grade began and my teacher was such a straight shooter his name was Mr. Varteresian he served time in the military and ran the class as such. We couldn't have parties in the classroom like the other kids and were forced to recite poems in front of the class. He developed a point system to reward us for doing well in class and always made us stand at attention as if we were in the armed forces upon the conclusion of class prior to the bell ringing to let us out of school.

At the time he gave us all a number and would call us based on that mine was number 5. He also had a little room at the back of the class that he called the Turkey Farm. If you ended up in this room, you would have to bring graph paper and write your initials in the squares until the teacher came to get you.

Typically, you would be confined to this room for talking in class and let me tell you I spent many days there because I liked to talk a lot in class. Although I knew the price, I would have to pay for talking in class I still ran the risk. Eventually, I smartened up and kept my mouth closed, and did as I was told. Although Mr. V was tough on us, he instilled in us many great values that at the time we didn't know we would need to fall back on later in life. Through much of the guidance of my 4th-grade teacher I started entering into spelling B's and boy was I good at it. I competed against many of the 4th graders in my class and, also won some awards. I was able to discover a hidden talent I never knew that I possessed. The school year was flowing just the way I needed it to, but many days thinking about my sister and was always anxious to get home to see how her day went. The 4th-grade school year ended, and I was soon off to the 5th grade once the Summer school vacation ended. All I kept saying to myself is that I hope the school year fly by so I can graduate and go off to the 6th grade and join my sister at the Thompson. Upon starting the 5th grade all, I kept thinking about was how tough Mr. V was on us in the 4th and saying to myself man I am not going to miss that. To my surprise, my new 5th-grade teacher ended up getting really cool with Mr. Varteresian and started running his 5th-grade class similar to how Mr. V did. I'm like man this cannot be happening out of myself Terry and Michael, June was the only one who was able to escape the madness his teacher was Mr. Fitzgibbons. I was ready to transfer classes but at the time that could not be done so, I just bared with it as best as possible.

Thankfully enough things turned out to be pretty good. I continued on entering into spelling B's competing now against the 5th graders and making it to the finals at The Elihu Greenwood School in Hyde Park, MA. Back then I knew that I was pretty intelligent and once I hit the stage, I wanted to prove it not only to myself but to my school also. Unfortunately, I lost and felt pretty down in the dumps about it. Many of my classmates expressed their feelings of being proud of me to make it that far. I eventually brushed it off and continued on with the school year as it was moving by pretty quickly. Before I knew it I was getting ready to graduate from elementary school. My dad took me out to buy a suit for graduation yes, I said it right, a suit. Back then and still to this day, my dad was the type to dress very well and still does. He bought me a 3-piece pin-striped suit with a pair of black wing tip shoes and a pink dress shirt and tie. You couldn't tell me anything on graduation day my spirits were way up, and I was dressed to kill. After graduation June, Michael, Terry, and I walked home. We were all proud of ourselves for completing elementary school and looking forward to the next chapter of attending middle school. All I could think about was me and my sister reuniting in middle school I would be going to the 6th grade and her the 8th. During the Summer just the following of graduation my mom started letting me walk to the store by myself. On one particular hot Summer day, I asked my mom for $1.00 to go to the Farmer's Market and get a box of Fiddle Faddle back when I was a kid that was my favorite popcorn beside Cracker Jack's. I proceeded to walk up Hollingworth Street and crossed over to Cummins Highway and walked past a brick building. Out of nowhere in broad daylight, an older gentleman came out of nowhere and places a revolver up to my head, and, demanded money. All that kept going through my head was that I was going to die at the age of 11. I handed the man the $1.00 my mom gave me and proceeded to the store anyways although I had no money.

Upon arriving at the store, I just walked around looking at what I could have bought had I not been robbed. To this day it still amazes me that no one saw that I was on a very busy street that seemed to always have plenty of traffic. I circled around the store plenty of times until I built up the courage to walk back home and tell my mom what happened. Once I started telling my mom the story, I could tell by the look in her eyes that she didn't believe me when I said that I had been robbed. I guess at the time she must have felt like little kids always makeup stories and this little guy here is doing just that. Eventually, I just shrugged it off and didn't think anything about it. The next day I asked my mom if I could join karate school because I knew I needed to learn some sort of defense. My mom worked with a gentleman who was sin sei at Once Step Beyond and he was very good at his craft. Once I joined the school, he took me under his wing and introduced me to Billy Blanks, and brought me along to check out several of his tournaments.

Over time I felt myself losing interest in the karate class and my instructor felt like I had a serious anger issue. At the time I can say that I did because of getting robbed every time I would spar against one of my classmates all I could see was the robbers face and dwell on what he did to me. I couldn't fully understand the concept that martial arts was more so about discipline versus fighting and there was a time and place in which the art should be performed. After several months I went to my mom and told her I no longer wanted to attend karate school but wanted to get into joining the Boy Scouts. At this time, I am now at the Frank V. Thompson middle school I'm in the 6th grade and my sister in the 8th grade. As I looked around, I said to myself wow this is where my sister has been attending school for the past two years. The Thompson Middle school was a totally different beast from the elementary school I had just left. All I kept saying to myself is that I don't know how I will survive this school for 3 whole years.

I would look out the classroom window and see people getting stabbed outside and once saw someone get shot at. After seeing all of that I knew I needed to become street smart quickly, especially after being robbed at age 11. I enjoyed plenty of moments watching my sister in her music class sing with the choir which was orchestrated by Ms. Garrett and Ms. Scott. These two ladies were phenomenal Ms. Garrett had a son named Denton which I became very cool with and Ms. Scott had a son named Keech who lived on West Seldon Street in Mattapan with which I was friends as well. My sister and I rode on the bus #410 to school it used to pick up in front of the Port gas station which was located right across the street from where I was robbed. All of the students who went to the Thompson who rode that bus lived on Hollingsworth, Rockdale, or Rosewood street and some of the other surrounding streets as well as Rexford and Regis Rd.

Almost every day there was a fight either in the school yard or on the bus. You could sense the anger and tension amongst the students both male and female. The school year was moving along, and my sister was once again getting ready to graduate, and here I was again back to square one trying to figure out how I could go on in middle school without her. Although my sister is a female, she was very protective of me I've literally seen her fight boys f or giving me a hard time and I knew that is something I would be missing. I went home one day after school and asked my mom if I could transfer to Umana Tech in East Boston to start my 7th-grade year. To my surprise, she said yes, and boy was I happy about that. Although I grew up in Mattapan the kids that attended Thompson Middle school from that side of Mattapan were different. Many of them wore jewelry and the high fashioned clothing you could just tell they were ahead of their time and have experienced things many of the kids on my side of Mattapan had not.

And so the 7th grade school year began now I am attending school in East Boston a town I knew nothing about aside from the fact that Logan Airport was located there. My school bus picked me up on the corner of River Street and Caton. On the first day of school, I'm like wow the upper- class male students had mustaches and the girls were fully developed me being a little kid at the age of 12 surrounded by others aged 13-18. Umana Tech went from the 7th grade to the 12th and man was it an experience. Most of the upper-class students smoked weed on the bus and in school in the back hallways. Every day I went to school I was guaranteed to smell like weed or just inhale it on contact. I just continued on at the school it was huge we had a black principal named Mr. Anglin and a vice principal named Mr. Sachetti who looked like someone out of the mafia. Mr. Sachetti wore double-breasted suits and plenty of jewelry and looked like scarface but was a cool laid-back dude unless you got on his bad side. The school year was cool getting acclimated to the new settings in such a large environment meeting people from many different areas Roxbury, Jamaica Plain, Dorchester, Mattapan, and East

Boston. In year 2 starting in the 8th grade, I began to become more comfortable with my environment, but the problems started to begin at home. The fights between my parents use to escalate to the point at times that I knew someone would end up getting hurt. At the time I played my position as a child and didn't really know what the argument was about all I knew is that the drama would unfold on a daily basis.

My mom would take my dad's clothes and throw them all on the front porch and looking at that I knew once my father arrived back home all hell was going to break loose. Looking at the situation I knew my dad must have done something that sent my mother over the edge but never knew what it was. Often times it seemed like there was just a dark cloud that reigned over our home and I needed to find some outlets to escape the madness. My dad would always be living at the house at one point then out of the house, it was really dysfunctional, to say the least.

I got really cool with a dude from around the way named Charlie he was my right-hand man and Dwight and Eric. Dwight's aunt worked with my mom at the Federal Reserve Bank and anytime I and this dude got together it was nothing but trouble. I found myself signing into school and cutting class always going downtown to Teddy Bears and playing video games all day and then catching the Redline to Dorchester to hop on the green line to Mattapan. We would walk to Maverick Station and catch the Blue Line to State Street and then the Redline to Washington Street now Downtown Crossing. For the most part, my focus was off, and I saw myself spiraling quickly fast in a hurry.

My dad took me under his wing and had me working with him at Bradlees department store working for a cleaning company called Hub Cleaning. In doing so this boosts my spirits a little getting the opportunity to make my own money and buy clothes to keep up with the fashion along with the other students. At the time my sister was in the 10 th grade and she worked for the department store Bradlees as a cashier. Although I and my sister were both working our part-time jobs and attending school the chaos at home never ceased The fights began to get worse and a lot of my parent's anger towards one another started to spew over to me and my sister. One year on Thanksgiving it was storming out with snow my father wasn't living in the house he was living with his sister at the time. A knock was on the door and my mom always said never to open the door for strangers it was dark outside, and I couldn't clearly see the person. My mom was sleeping at the time getting her rest for the night shift. The knock on the door got louder and then finally my mom said Eric open the door my sister stood on the staircase and my mom was in the hallway. I opened the door and the woman said tell your father to bring me back my baby. With a surprised look on my face, the first thing I thought was that my father had kidnapped this woman's child not knowing that they were actually dating, and they had a child together.

    At the time both my sister and I felt betrayed by our father but really didn't know the underlying issue that took place between my mother and my father. Soon after my mother and father talked things out and my dad moved back into the house. All I kept thinking to myself was the fights between them before were bad they are going to get even worse now. I carried on throughout the school year just looking to keep my mind occupied and not have to worry about the troubles that seemed to be escalating at home at a very fast pace. The 8 th grade school year ended, and I purchased a ticket to fly down south to see my grandmother's, my sister stayed behind to work her job for the Summer. Although both me and my sister know there was a lot going on in our home, we never said a word about it. Just like any other kids we wanted to see our parents stay together and make it in their marriage and look towards living a happy life. After the Summer ended, I came back home getting ready to start my first-year of high school and my sister in the 11th grade.

The school year started off pretty well as I continued to attend Umana Tech and my sister Hyde Park High School. I was searching for an outlet to get into that wouldn't lead to trouble so my friends Dwight, Eric, and a kid named Bruce decided to join the baseball team. Bruce was a very mouthy white kid and was cool for the most part but sometime couldn't control his mouth. One day on our way to practice me and Bruce got into an argument and out of nowhere, he called my mother the B word. I was so pissed off that I punched Bruce so hard in the head that I dislocated my knuckle. My hand swelled up so much to the point that it looked like I was wearing a boxing glove. Of course, when I got home from practice my mom and dad asked what happened to my hand I told them that I went to make a catch and my glove came off and the ball hit the back of my hand.

The pain in my hand was excruciating luckily enough it happened to my right-hand seeing that I am a lefty. As the baseball season progressed me and Bruce eventually squashed things between us and became friends again, but I always had the revenge factor in the back of my mind. I really was never a fighter in school always the jokester looking to make people laugh but never a bully. However, if trouble came my way the way things were set up, I had to fight back or run the risk of getting beat up.

One day while in school the principal came over the loudspeaker in my classroom and ask me to come down to the nurse's station. Immediately after hearing the request over the intercom, I made my downstairs to the nurse's office. After walking into the office, the nurse said to me I need for you to take a physical for baseball. Although this seemed quite odd to me seeing the season had already begun, I granted her wishes. The nurse asked me to take off my clothes and leave on my underwear and socks. I could tell she was paying close attention to my body and the scars on my legs and arms. She asked the question "Eric how did you go so many scars on your arms and legs? My reply "I was riding my bike and fell into some bush and got scarred up.

Right after I answered a police officer walked in and at that point, I was terrified because I knew I lied to them about where the scars came from. After the officer's entry into the room, the questions came firing at me and my face began to sweat like crazy. The officer asked me the question "do you have a sister named Angela? My reply was yes, I do, did something happen to her they said no but she told us that you both have been getting beaten at home with extension cords and that is a form of child abuse. At that moment my gut told me that I would not be going home to my parent's house that night. Earlier that day my sister got into a fight at school with a girl named April and she pleaded with her school not to call my parents. After seeing the tears from my sister's eyes asking them not to call, they asked why?

My sister replied, "if you call my parents I am going to get beaten badly when I reach home". After, my sister's plea to not call my parents she was immediately placed in Foster Care. Here I was in the 9th grade not knowing where my sister was or if she was safe. Hearing the details of what occurred at my sister's school and then saw that I was being placed into the back of a cruiser and taken downtown. Upon arriving downtown, we pulled up to this huge building and went upstairs and they placed me in a holding Unit. In my mind, I'm like how did I go from getting on the school bus this morning at 7:00 a.m. to signing in to homeroom attending a few of my classes, then called to the nurse's station, hearing about a fight at my sister's school to now downtown. I sat down and spoke with a case worker and they proceeded to file a CHINS report. This was a court case matter in which the Juvenile Court tries to help parents and school officials with troubled youth.

The first thing that popped into my mind is that both of my parents were going to go to jail. At the time I knew a lot of their anger toward one another spewed over to me and my sister.

Although I could figure out why I just knew there were many issues in our home and the verbal abuse my mom and dad had for one another was uncontrollable and seemed quite hateful at times. After the report was filed, I was driven to the Department of Social Services to be placed in Foster Care. This entire day was draining and seemed so unreal to me knowing that I was about to be placed into a Foster Home with people I knew nothing about. Honestly, I hoped that they could not find a home for me and that I could just go home but unfortunately, the system didn't work that way. I looked up at the clock and it was getting late by this time it was about 5:45 I'm sitting in the chair tired from all of the events of the day. Finally, I was placed into a home on Browning Ave. in Dorchester at the home of a woman who was Haitian.

Looking around at the home situation I went from a bad situation to one that was even worse. I went from living on a nice quiet street to moving to an area that was filled with pimps, prostitutes, drugs, and gangs. The home in which I was placed was seconds away from Talbot Avenue. I worked a part-time job at Purity Supreme and would catch the bus from Roslindale to Mattapan station and then catch the bus from the square in Mattapan to Talbot Ave. The walk up, Talbot Ave. was crazy you could see all of the Cadillacs out there, women in short skirts guys with silk shirts and slacks with thick shades on you knew that there was some illegal activity taking place.

After my second night in the foster home, I came home after school and waited for my foster mother to go to bed then I snuck out the back door and walked to Blue Hill Avenue, and hopped on the bus to Mattapan Square. I hated living in the Foster home many of the kids there did drugs and carried guns and I knew at the time my foster mother was just all about the money she could get from the state. I arrived at my mom's house and rang the bell she came to the door and let me in I could tell that she was happy to see me and although I knew the situation in my home was abusive I still rather dealt with that versus being where I was. Moments later after walking into my mom's house a police cruiser pulled up and an officer got out of the car walked up to the door rang the bell and asked my mom if I was there. My mom replied yes and shortly after they placed me in the cruiser and took me back to the foster home. The whole time I'm like now I am going to have to hear this lady's mouth asking me why did I leave? I walked through the front door and she began to scream at the top of her lungs at me. Why did you leave the house?

What's wrong with you? Are you crazy or something? I just turned the other way and went to my room and lay down for the night. The next morning, I got up got dressed, and made my way to school.

Living in the Foster Home I no longer had an assigned bus to catch to school which made for a very miserable trip to East Boston. I went from walking down the street from my mom's house to now catching a bus to Ashmont Station from Talbot Ave, to catching the Redline to Washington Street Downtown and then the Orange Line to State Street, Blue Line to Maverick Station, and then walking to school. By the time I reached school after doing all of that traveling, I was too tired to stay in school all day and eventually left early went dowtown, and just walked around for the day taking a look at my life situation and still not knowing where my sister was.

At the time I was in a place where I dealt with severe depression and really didn't even know that I was dealing with that at the time because then it wasn't a big thing. After walking around all day, I decided to catch the train to Mattapan and go back to my parent's house it was early when I arrived probably like 3:00-3:30.

I talked with my mom for a while nothing pertaining to me being in foster care or the whereabouts of my sister because no one knew where she was. The lines of communication were very slim at the time there weren't cell phones or anything like that. I just kept praying that my sister was okay and that she was not being harmed or anything. It really seemed to me at the time that my parents were concerned about what was going on with me or my sister. My heart always felt like their love for one another overshadowed the love for me and my sister. After being at my mom's house for a while the sun began to go down and it got dark out. Before I knew it, it was about 10:00 and I knew my foster mother was probably looking for me seeing the curfew there was 8:00. A knock came on my mother's door it was the police again, and just as before they placed me back in the cruiser and took me back to the foster home.

Once I arrived back at the house, I could see the look of anger on my foster mother's face once again. As before she yelled at the top of her lungs screaming uncontrollably and at that point, I walked out of her house again and went back to my parents. I think she must have figured out at that point that I did not like living there and although things were not great in my home, I'd preferred living with my parents versus being there. Here I was back in the house living like an only child not knowing where my sister was and also facing the fact that I may or may not see her again.

I couldn't understand how our family was so broken up the way it was. Both of my parents worked great jobs we lived in a nice home and they both drove beautiful cars. I guess the saying everything that glitters isn't gold applied to us. As the school year progressed, I found myself skipping school a lot with my friends Dwight and Eric these were like my main guys at Umana Tech it was like we had all the same things in common we were smart but did a lot of dumb things. Many times, we would cut class after the 3rd or 4th period walk across the street to Lenny's Spa and get a nice steak and cheese sub and then catch the train to Cambridge to Lechmere. Back then they used to keep the Walkman, on display and we would walk in put the headphones, on, and walk right out. We were pretty bold and honestly at the time felt like were invincible, so we made it a point to go there every day and grab something and walk out with it. My mom would see me walking in with these new radios, Walkman, and say Eric where did you get that from? and my reply was always the same I bought it. At the time as mentioned, I worked for Purity Supreme, so it never raised a "red flag" but my mom was no fool she could smell bullshit from a mile away.

One particular day, we went to Lechmere in Cambridge not even noticing that we were being followed throughout the store we grabbed an item as we always did and made our way to the door. Before we could reach it the security of the store approached us and told us to follow them to the back of the store. I'm saying to myself this is not going to be good, Dwight and Eric were all contained and the phone calls to our parents began and all I could think was that I was in a world of trouble once I got home and probably would have made out better had I stayed in foster care but hey you can't have both right?

Once I arrived home the extension cords came out the beating, I took on that day was something that I would never forget. My parents were ashamed and embarrassed by my behavior. My mom would often tell me that I was hard-headed and wouldn't listen to anything both her and my dad told me not to do. At the time I really didn't get much attention from my mom and my dad as there weren't the words, I love you or the hugs and kisses telling me and my sister that they loved us. Strangely enough, I felt like the best way to get my parent's attention was to stay in trouble at least I could have an interaction with them at that point, and even though it was a bad one I was fine with that. Much of what I was looking for was love and support from my parents I wasn't a bad kid and although the things I did were not the best I had great potential to do better things I was just in a really bad space and continued to spiral downward. One day I bumped into a childhood friend of mine and my sisters named Nicole and she said hey Eric how have you been? I said not too good how about you? Her reply "well I've been in foster care for a few months now and your sister is in the same home. I felt like God allowed me to bump into this girl and I was overjoyed at the fact that I would see my sister again.

The first time I laid eyes on my sister after the separation I cried so much with tears of joy because I thought that I would never see her again. For once in a matter of a few years, I had reason to smile again knowing that me and my sister reconnected. My sister eventually dropped out of school after the 11th grade, but I continued my journey in school as best as I could. After my 9th grade year, Umana Tech converted to a junior high school, so I had to leave. My mom felt it was best to put me in a private school located in Hyde Park on River Street called Boston Christian School. The school required you to wear uniforms which at the time I really wasn't a big fan of. I would catch the M.B.T.A. bus on the corner of Cummins Highway and River Street. The time spent there wasn't too bad I met a lot of great people. I had a crew of guys I hung out with from there Jarius, Kevin, Rick, Julio, George, and Andre. These were my guys and prior to attending the school, I had a long lasting friendship with Andre and Rick. Even though my sister was still out of the house attending this school brought me some happiness although at the time I still felt empty.

During the school year, I started working at Mcdonalds on American Legion Highway in Roslindale. At the time there were two black guys who owned it, Tim and Jim and these guys cared a lot about how their business ran and also the employees. It felt like one big family working for these two they both possessed a great vision and the potential for others. At the time I was about 16 years old and shortly after I was promoted to crew chief and many others who worked with me did as well Hector, Shonda, Tenisha, the list went on and on. I didn't realize that these guys were setting us up for greater things but me having the mindset that I had at the time I couldn't see it. One night shortly after getting off from work I caught the bus home as I normally do. I'd walk from Mcdonalds to the bus stop located over by Bradlees and would get off by Fairlawn Estates and walk over the bridge to Hollingsworth Street.

As I walked over the bridge, I could see lights flashing at the top of my street from police cruisers. In a panic, I started to walk faster to get to my street and upon arriving at the top one of the policers said "you can't go down this street. I then explained "officer I live on this street at number 75 he replied back there has been shooting so you are going to have to wait for a few before I let you go down the street. The whole time I am waiting I am thinking to myself a shooting nothing ever happened on my block we were a village and every family on the street knew one another. Now my mind is racing with anxiety, but one thing I knew for sure my sister couldn't have been harmed because she wasn't even living at home at the time. Eventually, the police officer came over to me and said the young man the shooting happened at 31 Hollingsworth Street. At that point now I am counting down the house numbers in my head. My home was in the middle of the street on the right and all of the odd numbers were to the right and started at the top of the street from smallest to largest.

All, of the guys I hung out with lived at the top Ricky, David, Andrew, Damian, Terry, Mike, June, Eric a.k.a. Sam and Tyrone, and Armon. As I started counting the houses down before proceeding down my street with the clearance from the officer. It hit me like a ton of bricks "oh shit" 31 is June, Sam, and Tyrone's house. As I got closer to my friend June's house, I could see the sweat pouring from his father, his mom crying hysterically and every family at the top of the street screaming and crying. All I knew is that someone was shot I didn't know whether they died or how severe the injuries were.

I then was given the news that my friend who I looked at like a big brother Eric a.k.a. Sam was accidentally shot and died instantly from his injuries. At that point I fell to the ground and started crying I couldn't believe what I had just heard, nor could I figure out how it happened.

Eric was a low-key guy everyone loved him and was very popular not only in our neighborhood but in school as well. At the time he graduated from Hyde Park High School with a scholarship for basketball to Northeastern University. Eric's ball skills were phenomenal, and I just knew once he entered college, he would be well on his way to the N.B.A. he was just that good.

Unfortunately, due to the circumstances, Sam would never get the opportunity to attend his first class or semester in college. Although the shooting was an accident I could not help but have a huge level of anger built up inside of me and really didn't even know what words to give to my childhood friend June who had just lost his older brother.

The crazy part about this whole incident is that person who shot and killed him by accident was friends with him too which made it even harder to deal with. Roughly close to a week after the shooting it was time to attend the funeral and at the age of 16, I couldn't do it. I prayed and asked Sam to forgive me for not attending. At the time I was young and just could not do it as it saddened me to the point where I felt very depressed, angry, and felt very lost. Every time I walked past my friend Eric's house after his death, I relived that night coming home from work and it ate me up so bad. Here I was 16, and my sister was still in Foster Care and just lost a good friend of mine whom I looked to as a big brother. Just when I thought things in my life were getting better, they were getting worse by the moment and the skies above me seemed to be darker than ever.

Once things started to settle down a little all of my friend's parents decided that they were moving out of town. All of these guys whom I established a great childhood bond with were now all moving off the street. David moved to New Jersey, Damian to Georgia, Terry to Roxbury, Armon to Florida, Michael to Mississippi, and Andrew to Florida. Will a.k.a. June different group of guys to hang with Rick somehow vanished for quite some time.

Tyrone eventually moved and got his own place. All my friends were in the process of moving and we started to approach the school year. The private school I attended ended up closing down and I then transferred to Hyde Park High School. All the folks I left at the Thompson after the 6th grade ended up reuniting with many of them in the 11th grade. Once the school year started, I was approached by the football coach there, Jack Farrell, and asked if I wanted to join the team. At the time I was a big kid roughly around 6" tall and weighed about 260 so I was all in for playing. It was cool playing on the team but the only awkward part about it is the same person who accidentally shot and killed my friend Eric was also on the team and although it wasn't intentional it constantly reminded me of his death and how it broke up my neighborhood at the ones I hung out with.

We didn't have the greatest football team, but we had some great athletes. Tony G, Tony J., Andre, Donte, and Eric P. was just to name a few but there were plenty of others. I played both ways on defense and offense. On offense, I played left tackle alongside little man a.k.a. Ventry he was a cool dude who lived in Fairlawn and was the first dude I knew from around the way who had a 3-wheeler and a pit bull. One morning after waking up and getting ready for school I saw the news and Ventry was on T.V. and had been charged with murder. Here I was back at square one again saying dam, here are another one of my friends who I may not see for a very long time. Ventry played aside me as the left guard, and I was playing left tackle. I'd have to admit I missed having him on the team as we grew great chemistry when it came down to running offensive plays. I learned a lot from him and looked at him like a brother.

With all of my friends moving off the street and trying to balance things out in life and trying to stay the course with my studies and sports it was very hard to maintain.

During my 11th year in high school, I started dating my kid's mom Bonnie and eventually started hanging aroundd her way. At the time she lived on Rugby Rd. in Mattapan not too far from where I lived so it was cool. There were a group of guys I hung with from around her way D, Poncho, J.C., and

Cisco. All 4 of these guys were younger than me so I looked at them like my little brothers and treated them as such. Things started to get crazy again at my house and I eventually ended up moving out and into J.C.'s house. His mom was super cool but was no nonsense at the same time and ran a tight ship when it came to her home. After a while I found myself getting into things that I never thought I would like riding around in stolen cars and drinking Cisco and 64 oz. of beer. Back then Private Stock was the beer of choice I began to skip school a lot simply due to the excitement of riding around in stolen cars all the time and drinking.

    At this point, I was 17 and felt like I would soon drop out of school and would never complete my high school diploma. One night during the Winter months I and J.C. were driving down Blue Hill Avenue in a stolen Chevy Blazer and the cops started chasing us. I took off doing about 60 - 70 miles per hour and started to take a right turn onto Almont Street when the truck did a 360 and stopped. All I could see was my life flashing before my eyes and felt like we were both going to die that night. Once the car stopped, I kept driving and the chase was on by the cops J.C. told me to drive to the Mattahunt and we would ditch the car there and flee on foot. In doing so he ran one way and I ran another. I took off my triple-fat goose jacket and ran as fast as I could through the schoolyard and made it over to another street. Running out of breath I decided to hide on the side of a house and boy was that a bad idea. I saw the lights flashing and the K-9 dog came out and sniffed me out and I was arrested and placed in the back of the cruiser. As we were driving the cop said where did your friend go? I answered "I don't know" the crazy part is that as I was taken away, we rode right past J.C.

    Me being me I wasn't going to snitch on him and have him get arrested. He made it away without getting caught so it was a good day for him and a bad one for me. The handcuffs were on me so tight that one false movement I could have broken my wrist. Here I was being hauled in to Area B police station on the corner of Morton and Blue Hill Avenue once I got there they took everything out of my pockets and my shoelaces and then walked me down the hall took the cuffs off he had me get in a cell and slammed the door behind me. A good friend of my dad's worked at Area B and when he walked through that night he saw me laying down on the hard metal what they referred to as a bed and just looked at me and shook his head with a look of anger.

The next morning, I woke up I was placed in a paddy wagon and taken to Dorchester District Court where I had to answer the charges of auto theft. The crazy thing about it is that I never even stole the car I was just driving the car, but the charges were just the same as if I did. Judge Dolan ordered me on probation and ordered me to pay restitution. I was given my shoelaces back and my belongings and was let go. Once I got home I and J.C. laughed about the high-speed chase and the adrenaline that was running through us both. We just always looked for crazy things to get into and it was never like we ever tried to talk the other out of doing something foolish our thought processes were the same just crazy juveniles looking to get into mischief always.

One day, J.C. and a few others and I drove to Dedham and ended up getting another stolen car from the parking lot close to where Lechmere was located. We all know we should have not been out that way especially being teens of color during school hours that in itself raised a red flag but at the time we really didn't care about the consequences faced and felt like for the most part we were invincible. At that point in my life, I really didn't care what happened and felt very hopeless when it came to living life itself.

One of the guys we were with stole a car out of the parking lot it was an Oldsmobile and of course, I was the designated driver. Before we knew it, the Dedham Police were hot on our trail all you could smell was the rubber burning from the tires from all of the vehicles going so fast. I was so disciplined when it came to obeying the rules of the road that I started driving as if the car were mine using the signals to make turns etc. pretty, funny right? Eventually, the cops caught up to us. One of the officers grabbed J.C. from the back of the car and hit him on the head with the back of the gun and I saw blood rushing from his head. The other officer reached over the front seat and grabbed me by the collar of my jacket and pulled me straight across and onto the ground. I'm saying to myself dam this dude is strong and thought they were going to hit me with a gun also. Here I was once again not even a week or two later heading back to court to answer stolen vehicle charges. Now the situation is even worse for me I was already on probation at Dorchester District Court and am now placed on it at Dedham District court. This meant something more serious than I could imagine at the time I now just violated my probation.

J.C. was allowed to go home, and I was taken to Dorchester to answer probation violation charges, things just seemed to keep getting worse. My life at home with my parents wasn't the greatest so I moved out and here I was basically on my own and still had a dark cloud over me. The entire 11th grade school year was just a complete mess and I was mentally unstable doing and getting into things that I never imagined that I would. I was walking down Norfolk Street one evening and ran into a few friends of mine Rick and Shawn they were both cool dudes from around the way. There was a guy they were walking with that seemed kind of shady, but I never really questioned it and continued walking down Norfolk Street.

We started approaching Evelyn Street and bumped into a few friends of mine from Hyde Park High, Reese, Chuck, and Lester. All of us proceeded to walk down Evelyn Street towards Blue Hill Avenue once we hit the corner a masked man came out of nowhere with a gun and robbed my friend Chuck and another dude tried to snatch up Reese but he got away and edged his way into the store. I was standing across the street and the dude pointed the gun right at me and all I could think is man is this how my life going to end at the age of 17? After the gunmen left, I went into the store to make sure that things were good with the other fellas. Things happened so quickly that I couldn't remember exactly where Shawn, Rick, and the other cat there were with were standing at the time when this all unfolded.

Shaken up by what had just taken place I started making my way home and stopped and grabbed a 40 oz. of Old English to get things out of my system. Once I got home, I went straight to bed and cut school the next day, and just hung out getting into whatever I usually did. After school let out, I bumped into Shawn and he was like man you can't go back to HP. My reply "why not? a few of the dudes from Corbet are after us. I looked at him with an ill stare and was like what man what are you talking about. He said as soon as I got there, John and Clarke ran down on me and chased me out of the school they think we got Chuck set up. In fear, Shawn ended up transferring to West Roxbury High School. I remained at Hyde Park High the day after I went to school and sure enough, John and Clarke approached me and were like man why did you get Chuck set up? I looked at them both and laughed it off like are you guys serious? Chuck is my dude and in my homeroom, and I'm not into getting people set up. Both of them looked at me and were like aight, but the whole time I'm thinking to myself I have to stay on my toes throughout the whole day just because they walked off and made it appear that it was over anything that could happen.

The dudes that attended the school from Corbet were all cool with me they had a level of respect for me just as I did them. Being a street-smart individual let me know that I had to stay on point because that little talk in the a.m. could result in me fighting 10 -15 dudes once school let out.

The school bell rang, and classes were out for the day I made my way down Metropolitan Avenue to River Street John and Clarke were on the bus Vee, Boodah, and a few others. Most of the fights from my high school either started in the school or in Mattapan Square so although I was on the bus, I still was unsure if this thing was over.

Strangely enough, I got really cool with Clarke and John and started to joke around with them quite often in school. I guess over time they looked at me, like well he didn't run from the school and faced us every day, unlike Shawn. Even after the robbery of my friend Chuck I was still unsure if this dude who we bumped into on Norfolk Street had something to do with it. He didn't really seem like he was afraid and didn't make much movement at all once it was all over with.

Unlike myself, I went into the store to make sure my friends were good. To this day I still wonder that if he did have something to do with it, we could have all been killed that night.

The 11th-grade year was over, and I could not wait for it to end the streets were wild shootings every day, drugs sold on every corner, and pimping and prostitution were in full gear at the time. The mid-late '80s was a huge crack era and guys out there my age at 17 -18 were getting it and driving fancy cars like BMWs, Cadillacs, Cressida's, and Maxima's just to name a few. The Summer had begun, and I was still working at Mcdonald's at the time and preparing for my senior year in High School. Taking a close look at how the 11 th grade school year went I figured it was time for me to move back in with my parents and try my best to gain some sort of structure in my life.

The Summer had finally ended, and 12th grade began I had failed so many classes between the 9th and 11th grade I knew the possibility of me graduating on time would be slim to none. School started in September and I continued to play football as I normally did prior and the school year was off to a good start. I continued dating my high school sweetheart at the time and things seemed to become a little more normal. I still continued to hangout with some of the folks from around my girlfriend at the time way but not as much as I did before. School was the focus and trying to still find a way to strategically make up some of the credits that I had missed in the previous school years was going to be a tough task to say the least.

In or around January of 1990 my girlfriend came to me and told me that she was pregnant. I was like c'mon stop playing she said I am I didn't have any doubts that the baby was mine I just knew at the time neither she nor I were ready to have a child. She told me that she would come up to the house and show me her stomach and when she did, I was both nervous, scared, and happy all at the same time. Now I am looking at becoming a father and at the time my head was so screwed up from all of the things that I experienced from Foster Care to getting arrested in stolen cars and nearly losing my life at the age of 17.

One night my girlfriend at the time's mother called me on the phone and said Bonnie's water broke and she needs to go to the hospital. I went into my dad's, bedroom and told him I had to leave to go to the hospital because Bonnie was about to have the baby and I needed to go pick her up to take her there. At the age of 18 here I was in the operating room of Brigham and Women's Hospital awaiting the birth of my son or daughter. Feeling nervous and in suspense, I paced back and forth in the room as the doctors kept telling Bonnie to push, and before I knew it

On September 18th, 1990, my son was born and weighed over 8 lbs.

I looked at him with a smile on my face and said, "wow I am officially a father". At my son's birth, I was still young, stupid, lacked direction, and didn't know the first thing about being a father. All I knew is that I had a son and it was my job to do whatever it takes to make sure that I provide him with all that he needed. The following Fall 1991 my parents wanted me to attend college, but in my mind, I knew I wasn't readily prepared for that and honestly felt like I needed counseling to deal with some of the trauma I had previously faced. My mom came to me and said "Eric you are going to attend college" tomorrow I need you to go out and find a school to attend. Since Curry College was only minutes away from the house, I applied there. Just as I thought my grades were not good enough to attend and was denied entry. Now I am making my way back home to break the news to my mom, and she didn't look too happy about what I had informed her.

The next day I called up the Marine Corps and set up an appointment to have a sergeant come to the house. Later that week the bell rang at the house and I went to the door to let him in my dad was at work at the time and my mom was in the room resting. My mom was resting at the time and once she heard me talking to him, she burst out of bed and walked down the hall way ,and ordered him to leave saying my son is not joining the service. At that time, I felt like my mom really cared about my well-being forbidding me to join the service. In my mind asked myself the question of where the concern was when I and my sister were in foster care. The following week I talked to a good friend of mine D who attended Johnson & Wales University and went to Rhode Island to inquire about the school. I applied and to my surprise was accepted and went home to deliver the good news to my mom. We scheduled some time after to go back up to the school and discuss financial aid or other sources to pay for my schooling.

The day before leaving for school, which was a hot Summer day on Sunday, I went to go say goodbye to my son and my girlfriend at the time. I would typically chill with both her and my son and watch In Living Color and The Simpsons. It was getting late and was almost time for me to leave to get pack for school and prepare for college life. As I was leaving, I kissed them both goodbye and saw my childhood friend Bernard walking down the street on Rugby Rd. I said to him what's up B and he replied "what's up big E" Nothing much man, about to walk home.

Where are you headed? He replied "Mattapan Square I said okay cool I'll walk with you and we proceeded to the corner. Once I hit the corner of Rugby and Cummins HGWY my girlfriend yelled out Eric, Bud is crying and wants you to come back. Bud was the nickname we gave our son. I turned around to go play with my son for a little while longer. I dapped up Bernard and he continued to walk on. Before I knew I heard sirens and ambulances fleeing to a scene but had no clue where they were headed. To my surprise that would be the last time, I would see Bernard alive. As he walked up toward Fairlawn next to the wall on Cummins Hgwy he was gunned down.

At the time I was in total shock for two reasons one being why would someone want to kill him and two how was it that my son who couldn't even walk at the time pulled me out of that? B was a cool laid back, the dude who never caused trouble and just worked, went to school and stayed to himself. It's getting later now, and my mom and dad could hear the sirens as well and now they are in a panic calling around looking for me. I eventually left to go home because now I wanted to see what actually happened and as I walked closer towards Fairlawn all I could see were close friends from Bernards's neighborhood some crying and some pissed off to the extreme and rightfully so.

I looked on the ground and all I could see was Bernard's blood scattered on the ground and on the wall. His Boston Red Sox visor was on the ground and all I could say was DAM why did this happen and thinking to myself if I were with him, I would have been dead too. My son would have grown up fatherless and would have never gotten the chance to know me.

Although the college had started, I could not help but think about the fire that would be brewing around the way because of Bernard's death. After the first week of school, I came home to attend Bernard's funeral and it saddened me to look at the young man I knew from grade school in a casket. My deepest condolences went out to his family and I couldn't think of the words to say to his brother on the day of the funeral. It saddened me, even more, to see his brother crying and others from our neighborhood as well. I had to try to dig deep to get my mind focused on school and try to create a better way of life for my son.

Here I was a father and attending college and staying on Campus. My dorm was located off of Elmwood Avenue and was in the hood. I would look out of my window at night and see prostitutes walking up and down the Ave. The liquor store was conveniently located right across the street from where I stayed at Stephens Hall. My roommate Robert was from North Carolina and weighed about 170 lbs. this dude was strong as an ox. We'd work out from time to time and he could easily push 425 lbs. on the bench with ease. I was putting up about 385 at the time for 1 rep but for me that was a huge accomplishment. Robert would always want me to work out with him right after classes let out right before dinner. Living at Stephens Hall I met a lot of different people some girls from Georgia Tori and her friend they nicknamed Peaches, Warren from Stamford, CT, and a bunch of guys from New York Dinky, Rob, Tyrone, and Eric.

The college life was cool, but I really didn't get much accomplished most if not all of the local bars downtown had specials in the evening 99-cent pitchers of beer and 10-cent buffalo wings. If you had $5.00 you were straight that would get you like 2 pitchers of beer and 30 wings it was crazy. Many days after school I would find myself hopping on the Bonanza Bus in Downtown Providence and catching it to Back Bay to go see my son. My parents never knew I was going back and forth from school to Boston like that but at the time I missed my son a lot and wanted to see his face to make sure he was okay. For the most part, I put my studies on hold just to be around him more.

On Fridays, I would ride with my friend D back into Boston for the weekend. He drove a teal Chevy Corsica at the time and once we hit 95 North, I swear we made it home in like 25 minutes that car would run I tell ya. I'd come home for the weekend and spend more time with my son and check in with my parents and would return on Sunday. My dad at the time drove a blue Cadillac with a grey carriage roof, that car was beautiful. I'd usually drive back up and my father would come to the cafeteria to have breakfast with me at McNulty. McNulty was one of the dorms where we ate our breakfast, lunch, and dinner. It was crazy cool because the students prepared the food who was in the Culinary Arts program. I at the time majored in business and that was my main focus while attending school there.

After sharing a room with Robert at the dorm it started to become frustrating because this dude was using my stuff like my deodorant eating the snacks that I had and other things. I spoke with my resident director to make a room change and it was granted I ended up moving down the hall and around the corner from where I stayed. My new roommate's name was Eric also and we both share the same birthday, but he is a year older.

Eric was cool when I first met him, but he always seemed to have issues with dudes from New York, and several times I would have to talk them out of seriously banging him out. At the time I couldn't really understand it but as they say in time a leopard will show his true spots. I thought nothing of it and continued to be cool with Eric. Although Eric was a young adult, he kind of had the demeanor of a little boy as far as the way he dressed. I'd ride with him to Portchester to visit with his family sometimes which was on the borderline of Connecticut and NY. One particular time we had a rental car and went to visit his family on a Sunday on the way back Eric had to easily be driving about 70-80 miles per hour.

I said to him "man you need to slow down Connecticut is hot on the highway and filled with State Troopers looking to pull someone over. Before you knew it, the sirens sounded, and the chase was on "I'm saying to myself dam I just told this idiot to slow down, and here we were with the staties, hot on our trail. The first thing Eric said when he saw the police behind us in our rearview after pulling over is "I'm going to jail". I looked at him and said man please don't tell me you are hot and have a burner or drugs on you. He replied no "I have a warrant for my arrest". I'm like dude don't you know that you are supposed to obey all the rules when you have a warrant? The cop walked up and asked Eric for the license and registration and walked back to the cruiser to check things out. Before you knew it, the trooper returned and asked Eric to step out of the car and placed him under arrest.

The trooper then came back to the car and asked me for my license, and I gave it to him. He then went back to his cruiser and was taking longer than normal to come back. I was like please don't tell me there is something that I don't know anything about that will get me arrested. Shortly after, the cop returned and said to me you are free to go PHEW!!!! All that kept playing in my mind was that I was going to go to jail and a call would be made to my parents as if I hadn't embarrassed them enough with my prior behavior. I proceeded to drive back to Stephen's Hall and when I got there some of my dorm buddies were like where is Eric? I said man he got locked up for a warrant as we drove back from Portchester. They were like what happened I said man he was doing like 70-80 through Connecticut with mad state troopers out there. All of them shook their heads and was like that dude was bugging.

Eric returned to the dorm the next day and man did he look tired and drained. Nothing further happened to him afterwards he just had to pay some fines in which his brother took care of for him and he was good to go. The school year continued on and moved so quickly before I knew it my freshman year in college was over and really seemed like a blur to me because I didn't get much accomplished I spent more time partying and drinking than anything else. Once my mom saw the grades, I received for the school year she had absolutely no intentions of sending me back to school there. All I could think was that I went away to college and waste my mom's money and didn't get good grades, nor did I remember half the teacher's names upon conclusion of the freshman year.

In so many ways I was trying to tell my mom that I was not ready for college, but she insists that I attend but mentally

I wasn't ready. Dealing with trauma within my home and outside of it was something at the time I had no knowledge of doing. Back then I couldn't really sit down and talk to my parents about many things that I was dealing with, so I dealt with things the best way I knew how. In the Fall of 1992 I applied for College at Roxbury Community College and even though I didn't do well at Johnson & Wales University I figured I would give this school thing a shot once again. My parents told me that it would be okay if I attended school there, but they weren't paying for it and I was on my own. I was okay with that because I worked a job and was making my own money, so I had no issue taking care of the expenditures for my college tuition. Even though I missed the campus life I felt happier than ever I was back home, my sister was too, and I was able to see my son every day.

Attending Roxbury Community College was cool in the beginning I went to all of my classes and unlike Johnson & Wales for the most part I knew everyone who attended school there because most of the students were from the surrounding areas. As the school year progressed , I found myself drifting off and doing what I previously did back in high school cutting classes and hanging out in the lunchroom and kicking it with my friends. For the most part the only reason why I showed up at school was to show off my jewelry and the clothes I bought to wear at school. Back then I had a big herringbone chain with the virgin Mary piece and sported a flat top haircut and stayed in name brand gear from top to bottom. I was really feeling myself and many of the girls who attended school there thought I was crazy cool, and the dudes did too.

One day during the school year at Roxbury Community College I got a call from my old roommate Eric asking me to come to a party at Johnson & Wales. I drove up there on a Friday with my boy Will and had a great time catching up with some of my old schoolmates and this was also a great time for me and Will a.k.a. June to catch up by this time it had been a few years since his brother Sam's passing and I wanted to do something with him that would at least keep him in good spirits for the moment. Upon arriving in Providence, I saw Eric and dapped him up and asked how things were, and introduced him to Will. Afterward, we got in my dad's car one of them an all-black, Buick Park Avenue. The car was bad all black with the black carriage roof, burgundy leather interior, wood grain, and tru-spoked rims. I felt like a baller driving around in that thing and many who saw me in it thought it was my car because my dad would let me drive it whenever I wanted to as long as I kept gas in it and kept it clean.

We arrived at the party and I saw many of my schoolmates and when we saw each other we embraced one another. Many of them would ask the question why didn't you come back to school up here? My reply was "the life up here on campus just wasn't for me, but I am still in school I took a step back and decided Community College may be the best option for now. As the night went on, we partied up and had a good time and it felt really refreshing just to get out of my neighborhood for a while and see some old faces. On the way home driving 95 North to Boston the heat in my dad's car was blaring and I could feel myself getting sleepy, but I couldn't have Will drive my dad's car that was just a no, no. My eyes felt so heavy that they closed for a second and I felt the car swerve to the left my boy Will was like are you okay? I said man I am crazy tired. I had to turn the heat off and roll the window down to keep the cold air blowing on me to keep me awake.

God was with us that night all I could think of is us crashing and me totaling my dad's car and running the risk of costing both me and Will's lives. As we got closer to Boston, I got off at the Houghton's Pond exit which takes you through Milton and into Mattapan Square. Back in the late 80's and early 90's Milton was a forbidden territory for blacks. Coming off that exit may not have been the best decision, especially with two black young me in a flashy car driving in the late hours of the night. I dropped Will off at his house and kicked it with him for a few before leaving and asking him if he was okay. Things just never seemed the same stopping at his house knowing that Sam was not there anymore. For the most part out of our whole crew it was only me and Will left on the street, so we tried our best to confide in one another.

    The following week Eric called me up and asked if he could come down to Boston and spend the weekend. I said okay cool let me check with my parents to see if it is okay. I asked my mom and dad if he could come down to spend the weekend and they were both fine with it. Although at the time I was a grown man it was still my parents house and they strongly enforced the ruling you live under my roof, you follow my rules, so I followed that as instructed. The upcoming Friday I went to pick up Eric from Providence at another party I saw many of my friends so before heading back to Boston I stayed up there for about an hour or two just to kick it with some old friends again.

    I took Eric back to his dorm and waited for him to gather some items for the weekend in Boston. While he was packing up his stuff he grabbed his brand new Air Jordan's, a leather Nike jacket with wool sleeves and a leather trench coat. I'm looking at him as saying dam dude we are just going to my house we're not going to a club or some sort of fashion show. Eric was like man I just want to bring some of the new stuff I bought that's all. I'm like aight cool. Once we got into Boston, I asked Eric if he was hungry because Simco's on the Bridge was open he said no I'm not hungry and I don't have any money. In my mind I'm like why would this dude have all the flashy clothes but no money just as always I didn't think anything of it. We went to my house and I introduced Eric to my sister Angela and then to my parents.

Afterward my sister got in the shower and I went downstairs to talk to my parents for a few it was late probably about 12 midnight at this time. Eric was upstairs unpacking his stuff in my room, so I thought. As soon as I went back upstairs Eric was like I need for you to take me back to Providence I'm like dude we just got here not too long ago. He replied "I know but I have to get back" I told my parents that I was driving Eric back to Providence because he had something going on and had to leave.

As I started up my dads Park Avenue Eric says hey man let's stop at the place you were telling me about to grab some food. I said to, but I thought you said you didn't have any money. He replied "I found $40.00 in my jacket so are good to grab some food. Not sure if Eric realized at the time but the events of the evening just didn't add up to me. I tried by best to give Eric the benefit of the doubt and thought he had a real emergency because he left all his belongings at my house and seemed to be in a panic. We stopped at Simco's grabbed some food and hit 95 south and made our way to Providence. How I made it to Providence and back that night I will never know. As soon as I walked in my mom started yelling at me you brought a thief into our home. I looked at her like mom what are you talking about she said "Your friend Eric stole money out of your sisters pocketbook" I was like this MF I knew my gut told me he was up to no good but wanted to give him the benefit of the doubt.

Eric stole $40.00 out of my sister's pocketbook while she was upstairs which explained why he had money for food at the time when we left. I was so pissed off that he took my sisters money I gave my sister the $40.00 and told her she could keep his new trench leather coat that he left behind valued at almost $400.00. I kept the Jordan's and the Nike jacket. Me and Eric were roughly about the same size and height so all if his stuff fit me perfectly. Although, I was pissed off at the time the joke was on him because he played himself. I'm like this clown really thought he was going to play me but it's all good, I'll take a $850.00 win in merchandise over $40.00 a ny day.

About a week later Eric asked my friend D to get his merchandise from me since he lived in Boston and still attended Johnson & Wales. I was like naw D I'm not giving that clown back nothing. If he wants his stuff, he'll have to come to Hollingworth Street to get it. At this time, I'm thinking to myself now I understand why so many folks had conflict with this dude.

It became evident to me to see why the dudes from New York didn't get along with him and to think I kept many of these dudes off his ass and this is the repayment I get. I mean I wasn't a gangster or nothing like that but these dudes from his state had more respect for me than they had for him. Week after week Eric would keep asking D to get his stuff and the reply would always be the same tell him to come down and get it. At that point I really looked at Eric like a clown and come to find out prior to leaving school my freshman year he and I both went to a girl named Lisa's dorm room and he stole her train money out of her purse and said that I did it. For many years I kept thinking in my head like dam this girl probably thinks that I stole her money when I didn't. Through the grapevine I heard that both Lisa and Eric were expecting their first child and all I could think was I hope this dude does not do her dirty because I know he did with me twice.Once stealing from my sister and then telling Lisa I stole from her when it was him.

Time had past and Eric finally gave up on asking for his stuff and I didn't see neither Eric and Lisa at all.

The first year at Roxbury Community College was coming to a close and I really didn't have any intent on going back. My main focus was on working and taking care of my son. My uncle Robert ended up getting me a job working for Polaroid in Norwood through a temp agency with him. It was cool we worked nights from 3:00 to 11:00 p.m. and since he lived in Mattapan at the time he would come by the house and pick me up. My uncle Robert was a big dude and didn't take any mess from anyone and although I wasn't too much smaller than him, I feared him but in a good way. On my first day of work my uncle had all of the guys who worked with us on the assembly line form a circle and then he looked over at me and pointed saying that's my nephew Eric and if you f&ck with him you have to f &ck with me.

Instantly these guys became real cool with me and there were never any issues. It was cool riding to work and working the same shift with my uncle Robert he was like a father to me and an uncle at the same time. Often times if I acted out my mom would tell him because she knew the fear factor would kick in once I knew that he was coming to talk to me. Over time an early shift opened up, and I started working from 7:00 to 3:00 and my uncle continued working nights. Working the early shift was cool because my friend Sam's mother worked the early shift and my friend who killed him by accident mom worked early also. It was good to see how much of a forgiving heart Sam's mom had for what happened to her son. I couldn't even begin to imagine how both of these women felt because could describe the anguish and pain I saw on Sam's mother face the night he was killed.

As I started to get acclimated to working the earlier shift, I began to establish a new setup friends Troy, Kevin, Leroy and an older cat named Rick worked the 1st shift. Troy was a cool cat from Lenox Projects and owned an Alpha Romero back then if you had this car you were like a superstar. Me and Troy got super cool and he started coming to pick me up for work in his Honda Accord every day after work the car would be filled with weed smoke. Troy loved to spark up a blizz on the way home and eventually I started smoking also. At the time I was like I can't go in the house with weed smoke on me my parents would kill me so I always timed it just right my dad worked from 3:00 to 11:00 and moms worked nights so she would be in bed by the time I got home. I just couldn't go straight home I'd have to stay out for a little while to give my mom time to head to bed.

After a while I started to call out of work and eventually ended up losing my job at Polaroid seeing that it was a temp assignment there was no tolerance for "call outs"

Eventually, my mom got super pissed off that I lost my job and my dad did too. It wasn't ultimately pleasing to my uncle knowing that he landed me this job and I just lost it that quick. The arguments between my mom and dad began again and the more they fought the angrier they became at me and my sister. I ended up moving out of the house again but this time I moved with my girlfriend and her family at the time it was her dad, mother 3 sisters and brother living in the home. I was older than all of her sibling, so I felt like the big brother to them all and protected them as such also. Here I was again out of the house and this time my sister was at home with my parents. I eventually ended up landing a job bringing mentally challenged adults to a day program and the job wasn't back, but it came with many challenges.

Each person who worked for the company was in charge of monitoring their own adult and if you took your eyes off them for a moment and did not pay attention to detail the ride home could turn into a horror show. The best-behaved adult sat in the front seat of the van and she was the easiest to deal with just full of laughter and enjoyed life. Michelle on the other hand who I had to monitor had some serious issues internally that she was dealing with. Every time we pulled up to Michelle's home in East Boston, I would have to get off the van go inside the house and get her. I could always tell by Michelle's demeanor if it were going to be a good day on the van or not.

At the time she had lost some family members and it caused her to battle things from an emotional standpoint like I had never seen in my life. Getting on the van with Michelle I would always have to hug her from behind tightly she had a thing with grabbing women's hair and would be in a rage when doing it.

Michelle was extremely strong and even at my size some days were more challenging than others to keep her under control. One day picking up all of the adults from the program I was getting on the van with Michelle and one of the directors was saying bye to me and I took my arms off Michelle for a split second and she grabbed the woman in the front seats hair she was screaming and crying so loud as Michelle tugged at her hair. In a panic I needed my co-workers to assist me and it took quite some time to get the two apart, but we eventually did. After that the driver who was like a supervisor to us all cussed me out so bad like I had never been yelled at like that before in my life but all in all it was my fault so I had to deal with the consequences.

As time went on my probation officer from Dorchester Court and Dedham Court kept sending letters to my mom's home stating that I violated probation and there was restitution to be paid for the stolen cars. Back then my mind was set on not paying the court and not checking in with my probation officers. I ended up going to Dedham Court and paying them their full amount of money but with Dorchester Court I appeared in front of judge Dolan again and boy oh boy if looks could kill. He looked at me and said Eric I am going to place you on 1 year stay of execution you violate probation one more time I am sending you to the house of correction.

As always, I nodded my head and said okay checked back in with my Probation Officer on the way out. My probation officer at the time Mr. Skinner said Eric what's wrong with you? You know this is the final straw right? My reply 'yes I know but not really know what stay of execution meant. In my mind, I'm like it's whatever my life continues to go downhill so whatever happens, happens. I continued to work my job and checked in with my probation officer a few times and paid my restitution for the stolen car. It wasn't much but at the time I really wasn't trying to give up my bread like that.

As time went on, I continued to disobey everything the judge told me. I wasn't checking in as I should have nor paying the fines as instructed. My probation officer called me up on the phone and said I'm surrendering you to the court for violation of your probation. Before I knew it, I was in front of the same judge that told me that I was placed on a stay of execution. He looked over at me and shook his head in anger. The judge said Mr. Jones do you know why you are here I replied "yes" he said to me you know I am sending you to South Bay House of Correction right? In my mind back then I'm like this guy can't be serious. He ordered the court officers to take me downstairs to a holding cell and still in my mind I'm like he's going to call me upstairs and this whole thing will be over he'll give me another chance and is just trying to put a scare in me. I watched the clock 1 o'clock became 2 o'clock and soon after 4 o'clock. I'm like okay there is one more hour before the court closes, he'll call me up soon and give me one more chance to get things right.

To my surprise, I was sadly mistaken 5 o'clock hit, and I and a few others were hauled off to South Bay House of Correction.

Still in shock but not worried about the situation I still believed I was going home and no one or nothing could deter me from feeling that. The next morning, I woke up it felt like a dream to me I was on a bunkbed with these blankets that itched like crazy. One of the C.O's told me to take off all of my clothes and put on a yellow top and bottom I'm like dam this shit is getting real. Thereafter they passed me a bag with a blanket, pillow, and sheets, and off to Newman I went. Newman was the name of the unit where it was a 23-hour lockdown and you came out for 1 hour for recreation. All the while I'm saying to myself dam how the hell did I end up here? For a long time, my life just kept spiraling downward and it was truly embedded in my head that I would be nothing in life and this would be the continuance of my life path for many years to come.

Here I was a father who lost his job, was now in jail, and left my kid's mom out there to take on the responsibility of raising my son alone. If there was ever a moment, I felt like I was at the bottom of the barrel in life this was it. After a week in Newman, I transferred to population things were a bit better over there as there was more freedom and I finally was able to swap out the bright yellow outfit for a red one. My stint there was very short roughly about 6 months, but it was a very long 6 months, but I tried my best to just stay focused. Often times my girlfriend would come up and visit me with my son and man let me tell you I felt like a piece of sh&t looking at him knowing I'm his dad and can't do nothing for him. At the time my son was about 3 years old and didn't really know much about where I was but still the fact remained , he and his mom were going home and I back to the unit.

Once I transferred to C.W.P. I knew that I would be going home soon and the light at the end of the tunnel seemed a bit brighter While in C.W.P. I got the chance to go out for the day and work which was cool because at that point I didn't even feel like I was even locked up although the fact still remained that I was. The day had finally come, and I was able to go home and let me tell you that was one of the best feelings of my life. Upon release, I was placed in a program that assist me with finding a job. I met this guy named Sanford who owned his own pressure washing company and I started working for him. You could tell once I started the job that he looked at me kind of funny as if he had trust issues seeing where I just came from. I always knew my work ethic so I told myself that I would just work hard and prove to him that I just made a bad decision and that I am a really good person it's just my background and the life I've lived thus far was not the greatest. Over time Sanford would let me drive the work van by myself and really started to trust me with his business. Sanford was a no-nonsense kind of guy.

He stood at least 6'5 maybe 6'6 broad shoulders and weighed about 280-290 easily and always had an intimidating look on his face. As time went on, he ended up hiring another guy and made like a supervisor. It was cool to finally get my life back on track and things in order and take care of my son and provide for him like real men and fathers should. We worked the auto mile in Dedham, Norwood, Walpole and would wash the cars at Lexus, Acura, Clair Honda and used cars.

Over time I started saving up my money and wanted to buy a car. Most of my travel with my girl and son we did on the train or walked so I felt as though it would be best to buy a vehicle. I ended up buying a 1987 red Chevy Cavalier the car was about 7 years old at the time and purchased in 1994 the same year I came home. The car was in great working condition the only thing I did to it was put a pullout radio in it back that those were called a benzy box. Things really started looking up I was working all the time Monday through Friday and getting paid pretty well I was only 22 at this time and didn't have my own place but I knew eventually at some point I would. I was still living at my girl's house, my sister was still at home with my parents and I was still trying to just stay focused on the goal of staying on track.

One day Sanford took me to Newton to meet up with a gentleman who owned his own detailing business can't remember his name. I was fascinated by the kind of cars this guy was detailing Lamborghinis, Porches, Mercedes, and BMW just to name a few. Looking at the guys in the shop doing this kind of work I started to grow interested in detailing cars and began to pick this guy's brain on how I could get started doing something like this. He gave me all the ins and outs of the business after meeting several times and also put me on to his distributor from which he bought his cleaning products.

He told me before I think about starting a business, I would need to write up a proposal. At the time I had absolutely no clue what a proposal was. One day I went to his office and he sat down and went over the proposal and outlined what it entailed. Before I knew it, I was out buying a wet dry vacuum a high-powered buffer, and other cleaning products. I didn't have money to rent a cleaning bay, so I decided to work right out of my car. While still working for Sanford I wrote up a proposal after buying all of my detailing gear and wondered who my first target client would be. At the age of 22, although I did many stupid things, I was pretty smart and already possessed a strong work ethic from my father.

I put on a suit and tie and walked into Enterprise Rental car in Hyde Park and sat down with the office manager and told him I was looking to start a detailing business. The rental car building was pretty small, but the manager was impressed by how I delivered my proposal and how confident I was in starting a business. Before I knew it, we wrote up a contract and I was offered to detail all of the cars they sold or rented to customers that they did not get time to detail. Man , let me tell you it was a great feeling knowing I just went from a bad situation and turned it into a good one. Now at this time I was still working for Sanford and starting my own business life for once I considered being great. E &J Detailing was on the way, I had business cards made up and a few shirts printed with the company name on them things could not get any better than what they already were. I was hustling like crazy to make up for the time I lost being away for 6 months.

One day I had driven to Mattapan Square to get a haircut and upon my return to my car my driver's side window was busted out. Once I approached the car, I could see glass all over the front seat, and immediately I thought someone had just broken in to steal my girlfriend's pocketbook or my radio since both were left in the car. At the time I didn't think anything of it and just went to have the glass repaired and continued with things. About a week or so later both of my front windows were shot out and I still didn't think anything of it. At that time the beef was on between Bel Nel and Greenfield so I figured someone must have seen me pulling up and didn't want any witnesses around, so they shot right after I walked into my girlfriend's house.

Back then she lived around the same neighborhood where the guys from Greenfield hung out. Again, I didn't think anything of it and went and had my windows repaired and went on about my business.

A few days later after getting the windows fixed this dude in my neighborhood named Steve pulled down Ruxton Rd. which intersected with the street I lived on at the time which was Rugby Rd. yelled out n*gga I'm going to kill you. I was replacing the taillight on my car, so I really didn't think anything about what he said and furthermore didn't think he was talking to me. I didn't have any beef around the way or any other for that matter, so I thought for sure he wasn't talking to me. As I turned around to look back, he pointed out of his car at me. I looked at him and was like who are you talking to? he said you with the black hoodie on.

    I knew of this dude growing up in the neighborhood but he was an older dude by the name of Steve his father was a cop and for the most part, what I always heard was that he rode off of that. Moments after he sped off in his red 5.0 Mustang with the black convertible roof. My first instinct was like I'm going to this dude's house since I knew he lived on Oakcrest around the way.

    I went into the house to get ready to head to this dude's crib to confront him and my mom pulled up in front of my girl's house and she could tell I was pissed off. My mom said what's wrong? I replied "this dude just rode up on me and said he was going to kill me and now I'm heading to his house to confront him" After telling my mom what happened she said to get in the car we will both go over there I said naw mom I'll handle it. She then looked at me with an ill stare and said get in the car we are both going over there. We pulled up at Steve's house his car wasn't out front, but we proceeded up to the door anyways and rang the bell. Steve's father came to the door and said to us both can I help you. The whole time I am saying to myself this dude's father is a retired cop and probably still has a gun in the house and we are on his property this is a huge risk for me and my mom.

    I then said to Steve's father "your son just made a threat to kill me and I want to confront him". His father replied back shortly after "my son said that you shot him in the arm" I'm like wait what?????? I don't even know your son like that I know of him but never had beef with him at all and shot him I don't own a gun. I'm standing on his front lawn like man this sh*t is crazy. I started thinking back to when the window was smashed out in the square and the gunshots after I walked into my girl's crib that was Steve shooting in front of my house. The following day the mailman came and there was a letter in the mail from Suffolk Superior Court addressed to me. I opened it and to my surprise, I was indicted for attempted murder. The whole time while I am reading the paperwork, I'm like this has to be some sort of joke so I picked up the phone and called the courthouse and read off the docket # and sure enough I was being charged with an attempt to kill.

The court date came up and my sister Angela took the Redline train with me downtown. Honestly, I wasn't afraid because I knew I hadn't done anything wrong. The judge called me up to the stand and read off the charges and then the prosecuting attorney began to speak and asked that I be held on $10,000 cash bail. I could hear my sister Angela screaming behind me Noooooooooooo!!!!! and then she started crying. I turned to her and put my index finger up to my lips signaling for her to quiet down because I know I didn't do anything nor was I around when this incident occurred. The judge let me go on a personal and once I started walking towards the back of the courtroom my sister grabbed me and hugged me tightly.

Once Steve caught wind that I didn't get locked up this made him even angrier that same night someone was shooting in front of my house at this point I knew it was him. In my eyes, I looked at him like a sucker because this dude had me wrapped in court, his father is an ex-cop but you are coming around my girl's house shooting. At the time there was absolutely nothing I could do my hands were tied and Steve still continued to smash out my windows and shoot in front of my crib. Several times this dude would see me on foot but would never pull up on me and get out of the car. At the time I just looked at him like he was a straight b*tch the more dumb sh*t he did the more frustrated I became and still couldn't figure out why this dude thought I shot him. My life was too busy, and I was making too much progress to fall into anything like this.

After the first date in court, the District Attorney started to read between the lines and started to think differently about me and was like I don't think you did it and will have the case dropped against you. I'm like cool now I can carry on with my business and continue to work for the pressure washing company. To my surprise, the DA was killed at one of the Orange Line T stations and the judge gave every person who was being prosecuted by him an evil grin.

Now I'm like dam first this dude Steve thinks I shot him and now the judge is looking at everyone who the D.A. was against as if there were a murderer. Now I'm like dam this situation is going to prolong itself for a long time because they will have to assign a new District Attorney, they will then have to review the case. I'm like WTF I had to go to court at least once sometimes twice a month and each time I had to take time off from work. In the beginning, my boss Sanford was cool with it, but you could easily see he was starting to get frustrated behind it. In my mind I asked myself the question "how could things move along so smoothly when I came home" and then BOOM here comes that dark cloud again?. It almost felt like on many days that someone was out to get me, or I would never be able to release myself from this dark cloud that always seemed to reign over me. Month after month the court dates kept coming and the more, I went to court the more Steve rode past my girl's house shooting.

After a while, I got tired of it and went to see my boy Kenny to grab a hammer. Upon arriving at Kenny's house, I sat down with him and explained the situation and he was like dam man. I and Kenny and were friends for many years so he knew me like a book so when I explained to him about the dude thinking I shot him he actually laughed because he knows I never got down like that. I started looking at the hammers and was like I like this one right here 9mm. after I picked it out, I got a quick tutorial on how to use it and was out. As soon as I got to Harvard Street, I could see 3 police cruisers flying up behind me. My heart was racing so fast you would have thought it was going to burst out of my chest. Thankfully enough after I pulled over, they went around me and proceeded on. In a panic, I drove to my house and parked my car went inside, and put on all black. Black skully, black Tims, black jeans, and a black hoodie and laid up in the bushes with the safety off patiently waiting to see if Steve was coming back through that night. After everything I had been dealing with up to this point it was either kill or be killed.

God must have been on his side that night because he never drove by my house that evening because I was waiting on him. Before going in the house, I rolled up a blunt and smoked just to calm my nerves a little bit because my adrenaline was on 1 million that night. On that night and every night afterward, I always made sure I kept the burner on me. It was crazy to think at the time I was never into gangs but knew many dudes from different blocks Chaos, Intervale, Castlegate, O.P. Corbet, Humboldt, Franklin Hill the list went on and on. I found myself having to move like many of them at the time because I was in a real beef with this dude. I was knee-deep into some bullshit that had nothing to do with me and at the time didn't realize I was in the belly of the beast. I continued working my job and appearing in court one month after the next. Each and every time I went in there the judge would call people to the stand and every one of them got locked up. The judge showed no mercy handing out 10, 15, and 20-year sentences as if it were candy at Halloween. Superior Court was very intimidating and many arraigned in that court were indicted for something or another.

One day one of the detectives in the Hyde Park Police Station asked me to come down there for an interview regarding this case I had with Steve. Back then in my early 20s, I went down to the station to see what it was all about. The detective took out a book of the surrounding gangs at the time Bel Nel, Lewiston, and Greenfield, and asked if I hung out with any of them. I was smart enough to know where the detective was going with this conversation, so I just told him I had no affiliation and the interview was over. The detective handed me a copy of the police report that was filed when Steve got shot and finally, I found out why I was accused of shooting Steve. This girl named Melanie gave up the wrong house to Steve which is what cause the mix-up. She told him that the person who shot him lived in a brown house on Rugby Rd. as soon as you turn off Cummins Hgwy. I'm like okay so Melanie just gave up the driver and not the shooter.

At this point, I'm like okay great all Melanie needs to do is tell the courts I didn't do it, and this thing will be over. Unfortunately, it didn't happen that easily because she said that she was scared to come into court and have anything to do with the case. Now I'm pissed off and went to her house to confront her which was right across the street from Steve. At the time of arriving to her house, I was strapped because I didn't know if I would see Steve along the way. I knocked on her door so hard as if I were the police there to serve a warrant. I was so pissed off that I had smoke coming from my ears. When she came to the door I looked at her and said how were you so easy to provide the wrong information but not willing to correct the situation. I looked at her and said "You know I'm facing about 10-15 years over some shit I had nothing to do with". The look on her face looked as if she really could care less and at the time I really didn't care about the consequences I would face if I were to pistol whip her.

As time went on from month to month, I was appearing in court watching everyone who was called to the stand in front of me get locked up and I go home. This all seemed like a bad nightmare that I just could not seem to wake up from. The more I went to court and was able to leave the more bitch shit Steve would do. I started thinking to myself this dude must be working with someone from around the way because I was always on point and watched my surroundings and oftentimes would circle the block a few times just to see if he was in the neighborhood. His car was bright red so you couldn't miss him but back then when people went on a mission, they would never use their own car and a stolen car would be the choice.

Eventually, my boss got tired of me going to court every month and laid me off. I was right back to square one all over again and it happened to be no end in sight with this court case. My son was getting bigger and needed more things and at this time my girlfriend told me she was pregnant again which was around the Spring of 1995. Now I'm like dam I have one son and another child on the way, just lost my job, and have no money coming in. The business I started was good, but it wasn't enough to keep up with everything I had going on at the time.

At that point, my hands were tied, and I was strapped for cash, so I began selling coke. Here I was in answering to charges for attempted murder, carrying a gun, losing my job, and now selling coke. I always knew that the two together would be a bad mix so for the most part I wouldn't carry the hammer with me anytime I went to go see one of my customers. Things were flowing just the way I wanted them to, but I always had to stay on point. The fiends would either try to play you or you would have to run the risk of getting robbed or getting caught by the police. Being a dealer came with a lot of risks but at the time I really didn't have a choice. I couldn't start a new job and tell them I was in court for attempted murder because I would be obligated to show up for work every day. In a sense, it felt kind of a good selling flav because it made me feel like a businessman and even though it was illegal. I had to do what I had to do.

My life at this point sucked bigtime but I had to keep trucking right along. I had a few customers around the way between Cummins Hgwy., Blake Street, Sefton and Ruskindale Rd. so I didn't have to go far to make deliveries. Most of the time I just did everything on foot because being in my car hot and dealing with Steve would not have been a good mix and would have eventually drawn more attention to me than I needed. Every night my pager would go off and I would be in and out the house to head to the pay phone to find out what was needed. I used to have codes when talking on the phone and would refer to the flav as being a cassette just in case the phone was tapped. I was already in court for one thing that I didn't do and most definitely did not want to make things worse.

One day a dude from around the way we called him Shizz approached me at the gas station on Cummins Hgwy and was like yooooo!!!! I heard you moving flav. My reply yeah, I'm doing a little something ya know gots to eat out here and things are getting rough for me. He said why don't you start fucking with me and grab product from me. Shizz was like man I can hit you off with some weight and just hit ol' boy that lives next to you with the loot when you are done. I looked at this dude like WTF I don't work for anyone.

After my reply Shizz looked at me and said okay cool we will meet up later on Tampa Street and I'll get you whatever you need. I think after that interaction Shizz looked at me like okay this is a stand-up dude who is not going to take any shorts. He says to me let's meet around 8:00 I said okay cool I'll see you then and I'll take a 8-ball from you to try out your product. It was roughly around 7:45 and Tampa Street was only about 2 minutes away from my girl's house, so I started making my way driving my car and had the burner underneath the passenger seat. The court case was still going on at this time and Steve was still up to his typical bullshit. I pulled up to Tampa Street and pulled over to the right waiting on Shizz to pull up. At the time he drove 4X4 Suv so that is what I was expecting to see. Before I knew it a Honda Civic pulled up in front of me around 8:05 or 8:10. I couldn't really see in the car because the windows had a very dark tint on them but I could see smoke coming from the tailpipe. The whole time I was sitting in the car I'm thinking to myself is this a setup and who was in the car in front of me? Immediately after having this thought, I reached under the passenger seat pulled out the 9mm and took the safety off.

I waited a few more minutes and there was no movement in the car in front of me. Somehow, I was able to see through the back window and saw that the driver had on a hoodie. The first thing that came to my mind was that this was Steve in someone else's car, so I proceeded to drive off. All of a sudden, the Honda Civic came flying up behind me and the first thing I thought to myself is that I was going to die and that this was a setup. As I continued to drive I rolled down the power window on the passenger side and thought to myself either I'm going to die or someone else is. On Tampa Street there was a point where the street widened to the point where two cars could fit side by side. The Civic got right behind me and then pulled up beside me I had the gun facing toward the window saying to myself whoever this is I am going to have to shoot them. Once the car pulled up next to me the person driving the car took their hood off it was Shizz. OMG I thought to myself dam I could have killed him not knowing who he was.

Once I found out that it was him, I pulled over. I could tell Shizz was pissed off that I did not get out of the car but at the same time I was pissed off too. He got in my car right after and asked me if I was working with the cops and trying to set him up. I'm like dude you know what car I was rolling in and you never said that you would be driving a Honda when we met up. So my reply was like dude seeing you know what car I was driving and you approached me about buying flav who is really working with the cops? I said man I have ¼ pound of weed and a loaded gun in the car do you really think I'm working with the cops. His reply was "okay man let's get this deal done and get out of here". I was like naw man fuck that and fuck you I'm good I don't need to buy weight from you I already have an ill connect. I told Shizz save that BS for the young cats around the way that fear you because I'm not one of them at the time I was in my early 20s and so was Shizz but he didn't know that. For the most part, I hung with a few younger dudes at the time who often looked to me as a big brother.

The whole night of these events had me on edge and definitely had me feeling like the world was coming to an end. Here I was again thinking about all of the things that I was getting into and the pathway it was leading me. Eventually, I ended up returning the burner back to Kenny and the first thing he asked was did I use it? I was like no, I didn't have any situations that I faced where I had to use it. We kicked it for a few and then I drove back home thinking to myself what if something happens tonight and I need the burner? All I kept thinking was that this would be the night that Steve ends up doing something stupid and I won't be strapped. My gut was spot on the day I returned the burner a day or two later Steve set my car on fire. The fire department and the police came to my house and my car ended up being a total loss.

Now I am extremely pissed and said to the cops I am going to kill this motherf&cker. The cop replied back don't say that we can arrest you for making accusations like that. In my mind, I'm like ain't that a bitch here I am jammed up in court over something I didn't do but they can't arrest him for something he did do. Time is moving right along and before my eyes, everything I worked for vanished right before my very eyes and I really started to feel hopeless about this whole thing. The one person who could save me in this whole matter Melanie was not trying to budge to get these charges lifted from me.

I started a job working at Store 24 in Mattapan Square on the overnight shift from 12 midnight to 8 in the morning a few days out of the week. At the time my mom had two cars so she would let me use one of them and I would park her car behind the bank in Mattapan Square prior to starting my shift. One night I went back there to get my mom's car and all 4 tires were flattened this had Steve written all over it. I never looked at him like a gangster because everything he did was a b&tch move and I could get over the fact that this dude thought he was a gangster but really wasn't. In my eyes, he was softer than baby shit and he proved me right every single time.

The week that my mom's tires were flattened I had to spend my whole check getting the car fixed and was in a no-win situation.

Eventually, I started to step my coke selling game up, I needed money and had to strive for any way to get it. One of the guys that used to but from me around the way named Chet was like yo man we should go down to Mission Hill I can help you make crazy dough down there. I'm thinking hard about going down on their turf to get off some product but at the same time thinking this would be a huge risk. One day I and Chet hopped on the 28 bus from Mattapan Square and started making our way to Ruggles Station. Going down that way I made sure that my clothes didn't look too flashy because that would have drawn attention.

Upon arriving there it had to be anywhere from 20-30 dudes just standing in the middle of the projects and my first instincts told me that we were about to get robbed. Chet said what's up to a few of the guys and then we made our way into the building heading towards the elevator. We got upstairs and Chet knocked on the door and this Latino girl answered the door very beautiful named Lisa and another woman was there too. I didn't realize that they were on the lookout for the spot and it was a drug house. Soon after being there for a little while a guy walked in and placed his gun on the counter, which looked to have been a 45. He looked over at me and was like young man I know you are not up in here trying to sell some product. I answered back quickly with the fear of getting my head blown off "and I'm not selling I'm actually looking to buy. In that instance, I had to think quickly not to blow my cover. He said what are you looking for I said a $20 rock. I passed him the $20 and he gave me the coke and after that, I was ready to go. There were some people in the apartment doing coke and I was like God please don't let this man ask me to smoke this in front of him. Thankfully enough he didn't and I and Chet proceeded back to Ruggles, After catching the elevator back downstairs to leave out of the building we had to walk across that group of guys once again.

The whole time I am saying to myself I know these guys are going to rob us this time or they will wait for us to pass them and then start shooting at us. Luckily enough nothing happened, and we made our way back to Mattapan Square. Dam that was a near scare and thinking to myself what the "HELL" was I thinking going on someone else's block trying to set up shop? In the '80s and '90s that would get you robbed, killed, or both. Over time I realized that selling drugs was not for me, so I stopped on my own and continued to work my job at Store 24.

Months and months had gone by and I was still going to court over something I had nothing to do with. My mom eventually asked me to move back home so I did at that time Angela was still at home and my mom and dad were going through a divorce. It was just me and my mom and my sister. For the most part, it was cool, but our home was still broken and so many different things had taken place up until this point. While living in my mom's home I was trying to think of ways to convince Melanie to go to the courthouse and clear my name from all the charges. It dawned on me that her baby's father Brian lived right down the street from me so the next day I went down to his house to talk to him.

I was like Brian your kid's mother has me wrapped in an attempted murder case and she isn't trying to go to court to clear my name. I explained the situation to him, and he was like Eric I am going to holler at her tomorrow and get this whole thing straightened out for you. Feeling relieved I was like I hope that this thing works as the next court date was approaching and it would be her words that could get me off this. At the time I hoped for the best but continued to expect the worst because that is just how my life was flowing at the time. On my way home from Brian's, I bumped into a friend of mine named Chris he was really heavy into Church and asked for my phone number. He said to me during our conversation "I feel like you are going through something" I'm standing there like wow how does he know that I am going through something?

I didn't think anything more of it he asked for my number and said that he was going to call me on Sunday night. The day I saw him was on a Friday so I was anxious to see what our conversation would be about in the next two days.

The next morning, I saw Brian walking up the street he said "Eric I talked to Melanie and she said she will contact the court on Monday. I'm saying to myself "yeah okay" and kind of closing my eyes as this thing will never be over. At this point, I was going to court for close to a year and didn't see an end in sight. The thoughts I had going through my mind is that this is really going to end in bloodshed. My next court date was scheduled for that upcoming Wednesday and I needed a miracle to happen to help me get my life back on track.

Sunday night Chris called me and said hey man how was your weekend? I said it was pretty cool and yours" he replied, "pretty good" and spent a great deal of the day in church. He went on to say Eric I have the feeling that you are dealing with something bad and I said back to him I am. After telling Chris this he said well tell me what's going on I want to pray for you. I said man I have a son and another child on the way and am in court for attempted murder for something I didn't do. He paused for a long time and said you are in court for attempted murder I said yes. Chris said man I am going to pray for you, but the prayer won't work unless you are truly honest about your involvement. I said okay and began to break down the entire situation from start to finish leaving out no details. Afterward, Chris said a prayer for me over the phone and ended the prayer by saying when you go back to court all charges will be dropped. I've always believed in the power of prayer and was hoping that this would work for me.

Wednesday came around and it was time to get up and get ready to go to court. I woke up ate a nice breakfast and took a hot shower, brushed my teeth, and put on my suit. I headed to Mattapan Station to get on the trolley to Ashmont to take the Redline downtown. Walking through the downtown area approaching the court which looked so intimidating with the wide steps out front leading up to the front door it made you feel as if you were climbing a mountain. The judge walks in and tells everyone to rise we all stand up and take a seat after.

The judge called one name after the next and each person who got on the stand went to jail the same day. As they always say whether a person gets time and how much they get truly relies on how the judge is feeling that day. By the looks of things this judge was in a bad mood I mean he just gave out time from one person to the next 10 years at minimum and 25 years at the maximum. Looking at my case the charges I was there for put me right at the median at 15 if convicted. Lunchtime had come and my name still wasn't called yet so just like everyone else I left out of the court to grab a bite to eat. While sitting down I kept saying to myself hopefully after the lunch break, they call my name so I can go home. However, the thought was still embedded in me that I may not see the home that day and possibly for the next 10-15 years. Lunch break was over, and the court continued.

Upon proceeding with the court, the judge continued right from where he left off locking people up and handing out extensive amounts of time. I looked at the clock 1:00 turned to 2:00, 2:00 turned to 3:00, and so on. Finally, around 4:30, my name was called and now I am feeling the anxiety build up in me because every person called before me went to jail. The clerk said my name loud "ERIC JONES" and said it with such force as if they were mad at me about something. I stood at the podium in front of the judge and he said do you know why you are here? I said, "yes your honor" You know that you have been charged with attempted murder correct "yes your honor". The judge then said "Mr. Jones we received information from a key witness at the crime that you had nothing to do with this" At that moment I could feel my eyes water as if I wanted to cry. The judge then said, "Mr. Jones you are free to go and all charges against you have been dropped" I thanked GOD. I felt so good that finally, this whole thing was over, and I could move on with my life.

   After arriving back home the first thing I did was call Chris and thanked him for the prayers and then walked down the street to thank Brian's house to thank him for talking to his kid's mother. Finally, I can now try to bring some structure back into my life and await the birth of my son or daughter. Taking a look back on my life of 23 years all I could say was dam I have been through a lot and seen a lot. In the Summer of 1995 my sister Angela, my girlfriend, and her boyfriend drove to Virginia to visit my uncle, aunt, and cousin. We were on the highway following in behind my mother, father, and my oldest son. The drive down was pretty good for all of us I and my sister's boyfriend took turns driving. We listened to Jodeci the whole ride down not too long prior to our trip the CD The Show, The After Party, The Hotel had just dropped. Both I and my sister were huge Jodeci fans. My sister would always get a great kick out of here me singing their songs because I would try my best to put great emphasis on it as they did.

   As we drove through the night the sun was finally starting to come up. The ride down in the all- white Lincoln Town car was the best. The sound system in the car was banging and the tweeters in that thing were kicking it was just us and the highway. We arrived at my uncle Johnny's house around sometime early afternoon around 1:00 or 2:00. The weather was beautiful, and we all rested up for a few and later on that day had dinner. My aunt went out and bought some fried crabs and we pulled the picnic table out to the driveway and began to feast it was such a great experience especially not having to worry about everything I had just gone through back at home. The evening was peaceful, and we all seemed to be enjoying ourselves with a lot of laughs being shared amongst us all.

The next day my sister and I were talking to my cousin Karen in the living room and she expressed to how excited she was to be going to see her grandfather in North Carolina. Both my aunt and uncle were from North Carolina, so I thought she meant her mother's dad.

I replied back "that's great you will be seeing your mom's dad this Summer. She replied back saying "no I am going to visit my father's dad. Instantly both I and my sister sat there with a blank stares on our faces like wait a minute your father is our mom's brother, so your grandfathers ours too. Both I and my sister looked puzzled in the face 23 and her at age 25 sitting in total shock to learn that our grandfather was alive. Neither I nor my sister ever met my grandfather before which left us with a mystery in our minds as to why our mother never mentioned him before. Both my sister and I knew that my grandfather on my dad's side had passed away prior to us both being born but were unsure why my grandfather on my mom's side was never talked about.

Although I was happy to hear that he was alive and that I would possibly someday meet him it left a tad bit of anger in me to know my mom would hide something like this from both me and my sister. Both of us traveled for many years flying to North Carolina for the Summers and never once from the time of being a kid until adulthood was there ever a mention of my grandfather. Our only hopes were to maybe meet him someday and get the opportunity to catch up with him and tell him all about us and the things we've accomplished or been through in life. We never knew when that day would happen or even if it would happen at all. After a couple of days, we drove to North Carolina to stay at my aunt Susie's house. Flying down in the Summer to her home were the best times ever as a kid and into my teenage years. My aunt could bake and cook so well and was the first person to introduce me and my sister to Red Velvet cake back in the 80s. Just the thought of it has me licking my lips looking for a slice.

My aunt and grandmother lived right next to each other and the only thing that separated their homes was a huge cornfield.

Often times as kids we would cut through the corn field to get to my grandmother's house. The steps at my grandmother's house had my and my sister's footprints embedded into the concrete.

Both my name and hers were in the steps with the year 1973 right next to them. My grandmother never had the steps redone and kept it that way for many, many years. We were both the oldest out of all the grandchildren my sister being the oldest out of the granddaughters and me being the oldest out of the grandsons. Despite all of the things that I have endured up until this point I never talked about it to my grandmother. I think for the most part visiting with her was a time for me to enjoy myself and not talk about all of the things that I have been dealing with from back home so I just left things alone and made the best of my time in the south.

I made it a point to get back down south and finally meet my grandfather for the first time. My aunt asked him if he knew who I was, and he just shook his head with the gesture of saying 'no'. To my surprise, he had no clue that I was his oldest grandson. Here my grandfather was standing before me with glasses on a long sleeve shirt and a pair of overalls. As I looked at him my uncles resembled him so much and every one of them had some or all of the same characteristics as my grandfather. He was brown-skinned about my complexion and slender. Still standing there in awe I couldn't believe the many years my sister and I traveled to North Carolina I never met him before. A big part of me wanted to ask my mom why she never mentioned him growing up but I just left things alone and felt at the time since he was never talked about by either my mom or dad that maybe something bad happened, many, many years prior. Back then it was always best for a child to stay in their place and obey their parents.

There was always a rule of thumb in my home if you were meant to know about something you will find it out about it much sooner rather than later.

Seeing that so many years had passed couldn't be mad at my grandfather because honestly I didn't know what happened and at that point me being older I really didn't care about what occurred all I knew was that I had my grandfather and that's all that mattered to me.

Upon my return back to Boston, it seemed like the rest of the year flew by and before I knew it, it was December 1995, and my youngest son was born. He was such a big beautiful baby and born with a head full of hair, and very curly eyelashes. Often times after he was born around 3-4 months, I would take him out and many people thought that he was a girl. Folks would always say your little girl is so beautiful and has pretty eyes. I would always reply back to them and tell them that he wasn't a girl, this probably went on until he turned 1 or 2. A few months later my girl's parent's house was foreclosed on which forced them to move out. At the time both of my kids were living with their mom and her parents along with her siblings. Experiencing everything that I dealt with up until this point truly resonated in me with the statement "when it rains it pours"

After the house was sold, my girlfriend and two sons, and her baby sister moved into my mom's house. At the time my sister had moved out and I can't really remember where she lived at the time. All I knew was that I needed to step my game up and get an apartment. I was a father with two kids and a girlfriend. I sat down and talked to my mom about the living situation and told her that we would be living there for two months tops. My mom looked at me with a grin and said 2 months I replied "yes". I said to her "mom I'm a grown man I can't see myself raising my family in your home. I got on my grind continued to work at Store 24 full time and worked for a law firm as a courier full time. Before I knew it 2 months had passed by and on July 1, 1996, I signed the lease to my first apartment. What a great feeling I had within me that day and it was definitely a blessing from above.

    I and my girl ended up getting a 2BR apartment in Dorchester on Dyer Street. Back then rent was cheap so I was able to swing it myself at $550.00 a month. The neighborhood was cool and close to where I attended school at the Frank V. Thompson Middle School. I applied for a job working for a manufacturing company called Plymouth Rubber and ended up landing the job. At that point, I was able to quit both of the full-time jobs I had as they both paid the same in total as the 1 full-time job I had just gotten. The pay was great and offered plenty of overtime and things were starting to look up for a change finally I could breathe easy with all of the bullshit now behind me. My oldest son was attending James J. Chittick School at the time and was in Kindergarten, my youngest son Tevin was just a baby so my girl's sister would watch him during the day for us and we would pay her.

    I started getting acclimated to the neighborhood and made it a weekly ritual to walk to the Barbecue Pit on Morton Street on Fridays and grab some beer to bring home. One day I walked to the corner store located on Norfolk Street to grab some snacks for my kids and saw a guy washing his car and bumping some S.O.S. Band. I walked over and introduced myself and he told me his name was "Greg" from that day forward we became good friends there was about a 5-year age difference between us two. At the time I was like 24 and he was 29 but I have always been one to hang with folks older than me so that was cool. Greg made me a few Old School CDs and I used to listen to them in my car every day on my way to work driving down route 138 through Milton in the mornings and heading to Canton.

After living on Dyer Street for about 5 years we ended up moving to Alpha Rd. in Dorchester in 2001 to another 2-bedroom apartment. I liked this place a lot at the time I had a deck off from the bedroom with a sliding door and had my grill set up back there to cook burgers and hot dogs for my kids.

At this time, I was driving a 1997 Volkswagon Jetta bright red with dark tinted windows and kept the car spotless. In 2001 they were starting to cut back hours at my job the checks that used to be like $800-$900 a week started to dwindle down to about $500 a week. Everyone in the company aside from the higher ups could see that the company would be closing soon. I took full advantage of the tuition reimbursement and went to school for Computer Technical Support at Katharine Gibbs School. The program lasted about a year and I graduated in 2002 with honors and made it to the Dean's List. Although I had a minor setback in pay things weren't too bad seeing my girl was working too at the time.

In 2002 I took on a job working at Beth Israel Deaconess Medical Center in Brookline as an Operating Room attendant. This wasn't the cleanest job, but I saw things going bad at my previous employer, so I had to make some changes to keep money coming in to keep a roof over all 4 of our heads. My hours were from 7-3 just like at Plymouth Rubber but I didn't work nearly as hard as the job I held at the time was a little bit more laid back. Within the same year, I was promoted to a position called Material Handler and was responsible for keeping all of the necessary operating room supplies stocked in all of the pods. Once I got a feel for the position and learned my job well I could literally knock it out in about 3 to 4 hours and have the rest of the day to either walk around or just chill in different departments and visit with some friends I met there. I was required to carry a pager, so the staff always had a way of getting in touch with me if they needed something.

In early 2003, I was promoted again and started working as a Material Manager for the operating room. This position required me to work from 6:00 a.m to 2:00 a.m. which I didn't mind at all.

The hours were perfect I would park my car at Whittier Street projects cross the street to Ruggles Station and then catch the shuttle to the medical district.

A couple of months later my girlfriend was pregnant again and at the time my sons were turning 8 and 13 that year. All I kept thinking is that we are having another child and were hoping for a girl this time not that I didn't love having boys I just wanted a girl this time around. Months would go by and I would eat out with my sons all the time and would be putting on so much weight due to not eating healthy. Finally, the month of November came and it was time for my girlfriend Bonnie to go into labor, I drove her to Brigham & Women's Hospital which was conveniently located right around the corner from where I worked at the time. After work I would go over to the hospital and stay the night just in case, she had the baby in the late hours of the night.

One day while I was at work, I got a call from the hospital saying that Bonnie's labor would be induced. I went over to the hospital and the doctors and nurses began working on her and before I knew it, I was the proud father of a baby girl. My wish had come true to have a little girl and I had vowed that I would keep the bond between her and me pretty tight. She was such a little peanut when she was born and the smallest out of my 3 kids at birth. The next day when I went to work all of my co-workers congratulated me and my family on our new addition. My girl stayed home for about a few months on maternity leave and once she went back to work, I stayed home with my daughter during the day. My boss at the time Bob was crazy cool he allowed me to come to work at night and do my job and still paid me for 40 hours. This worked out so well for us because I couldn't think of a babysitter at the time for my daughter nor did I want her going to daycare until she was at least 6 months or so, so we held off on sending her to daycare.

As we became accustomed to the neighborhood, we came across a lady in or about her mid to late 40s who offered babysitting services. She was a Latino woman who was very nice and cared very much for the kids she watched. Prior to letting her babysit my daughter we both went by her house just to observe how she was with the kids and instantly I/we were impressed. Alyssa started going there roughly around the age of 4-5 months and actually liked going so that put us more at ease when we dropped her off.

One Sunday a friend of mine had some playoff tickets to go see the Boston Celtics play as they were trying to advance to the finals. I and my friend Wayne hopped on the train and headed down to North Station to check out the game. The Celtics were playing against the Indiana Pacers so we both knew that it would be a great matchup. The game was exciting and went back and forth for 4 quarters with the Pacers eventually winning the game. I've always been a huge Boston fan for all of our teams so you would never see me rooting for the opposer. Upon arriving back home I asked my girlfriend where my sons were. and she replied "down the street playing at the park at Fields Corner"

I've always forbade my sons from going down to that park by themselves, especially with all the gun violence and gang activity still very much alive and well. I started pressing my scrubs for work the next day and for some reason I had a funny feeling come over me. Something from within spelled out trouble but I couldn't put my finger on what it could be. Before I knew it, my oldest son called me from his cell phone and said dad these people are down here beating us up. I said to him by who? At the time my oldest was 13 and my youngest 8 so in my mind, I'm like kids will be kids and will make stuff up. Then my youngest son took the phone from my oldest and he was crying so loud I couldn't even make out what he was saying.

In a panic, I threw on a pair of pants jumped in my Dodge Intrepid, and made my way down to the park. When I pulled up, I saw this black lady pointing at my oldest son's face. I could see blood coming from close to where my son's left eye was. I'm like wtf is going on here? The lady replied back "your kids were bothering mine, so my kids beat yours up". Then she went on to say if you want some my son will come down here and kick your ass too. I looked at her and laughed and said your son isn't going to do shit. She fired back at me saying if I call him, he will whip your ass. At the time I had on house slippers and a pair of scrubs. I looked at her and said I'm going to go home and change and when I come back all hell is going to break loose. She continued to come out of her mouth like crazy c'mon back we got something for you. I'm like alright et I'll be right back.

Looking at the blood coming from my youngest son's head pissed me off to no extent. My oldest son had a knot on his forehead and is the protector of my family that I am it made me even more pissed off. My youngest son's skin by his eye was busted open you could see the white meat, this lady's son hit my son in the face with a steering wheel that he found in the park. Her daughter who was like a tomboy punched my oldest son in the forehead which made it swell up.

I raced back to the house and changed my clothes and while getting dressed all I could think to myself I am going to jail today. I told my girlfriend to take my sons to the hospital and I would handle the family, but my youngest son started crying and didn't want to leave me for the fear that I might get hurt. Driving back down to the park full of rage and my girlfriend following with my sons in the car I don't even think my car was fully in park. I jumped out of my car and this entire woman's family was there a few dudes, the girl who punched my oldest son, the mother, and an aunt. My first words were where the f*ck is your son she said "there he is over there"

I walked up to him and said so what's up I heard you're supposed to be kicking my ass.

I walked up to him and said "so what's up I heard you're supposed to be kicking my ass" and before he could reply I stole on him so hard that he fell backward to the ground. The sister who hit my son was mad and started to make her way toward me, so I pushed her to the ground.

Before I knew it, about 3 to 4 police cruisers showed up and one of the cops jumped out of his cruiser and tried to grab my wrist. A few of their family members were getting pissed off because I came back with a force and was handling their whole family like a champ. The other two dudes who were friends just stood there. I'm like these dudes have to be straight-up suckers because there is no way I would let one dude steal on my man knock him out and not jump in.

The sister who was a tomboy punched the windshield to one of the cruisers and shattered the entire glass. I was like dam I know for sure she is going to jail and once this brawl is over, I know I am too.

Eventually, the brawl came to a cease and the officer placed the cuffs on me, and off to the police station I went. I really didn't feel bad about my behavior because I was doing what any loving father would do and that was to protect my children. While at the police station you could hear the sister, who shattered the windshield say man we are going to see you in the streets and we're coming for you. I laughed like whatever you ain't going to do sh*t. After about 2 hours I ended up getting bailed out of jail and rushed home to make sure my boys were okay. Prior to leaving the station, the officer informed me that I would have to go to Dorchester District Court the next morning. My youngest son Tevin had to get stitches at Carney Hospital and my oldest just iced down his forehead until the swelling was gone. I was really relieved to see them both and know that they were okay.

The next day I went to court and had to answer charges of assault and battery. Of course, the way that the judicial system runs at times made it appear as though I was the one in the wrong. At the time maybe I was and should have just walked away and pressed charges but at the moment, I was just filled with rage after what happened to both of my sons. Back then at the time, I wasn't one to really weigh out the consequences I was more so an, I'll act not and face the consequences later kind of thinker. The mother got up on the stand and told the judge I needed to be tested for steroids, I laughed at her comment like "steroids I never touched them a day in my life". I don't think she really knew that she woke up the beast with her comment of having her son kick my ass.

Finally, I got the opportunity to tell my side of the story simply explaining that my kids were at the park at Fields Corner and her kids started messing with them and it turned violent. The judge initially just threw the case out and no one was charged with anything which was weird to me seeing that my son had to get stitches and the tomboy of a girl punched my oldest son on the forehead. After court was over me and my family went home but from that moment forward, I wouldn't allow my kids to go to the park under any circumstances. It was crazy to think that I couldn't even let my kids go to the park and play. Back when I was a child we could always go to the park and not have to worry about any issues and here I was trying to find different outlets for my sons because I know they loved to go to the park and play basketball. Shortly after this incident, I lost one of my youngest cousins on my dad's side "Rich" 2004. Rich was attending college in Buffalo, New York at Canisius on a 4-year scholarship for basketball. I remember my dad calling me on the phone and giving me the news and couldn't believe what my ears were hearing. I've always looked at my cousin Richard like a little bother more so than a cousin. He was 11 years younger than me and had passed away at the age of 21.

Rich collapsed on the basketball court during practice one day and when I received the news from my father I was in total disbelief. Rich was such a young and vibrant individual and although he was younger than me, I looked up to him and always thought to myself why couldn't I be more like him at his age? I guess since our surroundings were different which played a huge part in it all. As time progressed, I found myself always feeling sad and somewhat depressed.

There were many days I would head to work, park my car at Whittier Street projects as I normally would do, and just sit in my car and let out a loud cry before going to Ruggles Station to catch the shuttle work.

At this point in my life, I knew that things would not be the same at all because there was a huge part of my life missing. The crazy part about it all is that my youngest son resembled Richard so much in the face especially when Rich was a young kid like my son. As always, I tried to find a way to gain some true happiness in life because it always seemed to pour rain no matter the situation, and never seemed like the end was coming.

Shortly, after I began dipping and dabbling into some medical supply sales which were legal, but I was getting them from someone who had stolen the stuff and bought it at a wholesale price.

Before I knew it was making so much money some weeks $5,000 other weeks twice that amount and in doing this it made me start to feel happy but only for the moment. As they say, money is the root of all evil and that saying proved itself over time. 2004 kept moving along right after my cousin's death and I found myself making a lot of money and spending it just as quick as I made it. I furnished my whole apartment, bought my girlfriend a new van, and bought myself a Lincoln Navigator. My SUV was hooked up well I had a Kenwood System, a DVD player for my kids with wireless headphones. The truck was like a living room on wheels, well that's what I used to call it.

In early 2005, I proposed to my girlfriend and married her in August. The wedding was great and although I and my girlfriend had our share of ups and downs as a man and father, I wanted to do the right thing by keeping my family together. Looking at many of the issues both of our parents had we tried our best to change the dynamics. Our wedding was great we had at least 24 people in our wedding party which consisted of close friends and family. The church we got married in was located on Commonwealth Avenue in Boston and the reception was held at Lantana's in Randolph

For the bridesmaids, we had a stretch Ford Excursion and for the guys, we had a stretch Hummer with a black top. The eye-catcher of the day was when I and my wife got into a pearl white 1947 Rolls Royce and drove away from the church. So many strangers stopped and took pictures of us both and really had us feeling like we were celebrities. We both toast a glass of wine and smiled to begin our journey as husband and wife.

At the wedding reception, our D.J. played some soft music and the cocktail hour began. We had an open bar for our guest's scallops wrapped in bacon, chicken wings a cheese and cracker tray, etc. If there were any time in life where I felt like I was on top of the world during this time was it and I was ready for this new chapter of life. By this time prior to getting married me and my girlfriend were together for 16 years our kids would be turning 2, 10, and 15 after we married. After marriage, we decided to move to Quincy to give our kids a better life surrounding them. My kids adjusted pretty well my daughter continued with her daycare in Dorchester, my oldest son was at the John D' O'Bryant and my youngest son was still attending school at the James J. Chittick. In September of 2006, I quit my job at Beth Israel Deaconess and started working for the M.B.T.A. Massachusetts Bay Transit Authority.

The job was cool when I first started, the people there were cool, and the job paid great. I started out working part-time but in less, than 3 months began working full time and was eligible for overtime. After a while, I started to dislike working there because the place seemed like a big high school because there was so much gossip amongst the men which was not something I was into. About or around May of 2009 I ended up getting arrested by Federal Agents for the illegal activity that I was caught up with. In doing so this caused me to lose my job and at the time I was really worried not only about the court case but how was I going to feed my family also. Just as I thought things were getting better, they were getting worse and I had no clue as to how I would bounce back from this one. I was stressing out and drinking pretty heavily I mean it was nothing for me to down a pint of Hennessey at like 9:00 or 10:00 in the morning I guess you could say I started developing the same habits that of a drunk.

As my court case went on in Federal Court, I would set up an appointment to meet with my attorney to see if there was anything I could do to get off. I mean the cards were stacked against me so hard. The feds took the computers from my home and my phone to trace all of the transactions that I had done. I had people I was dealing with in China, Florida, Michigan, and Georgia and kept my clients happy always because the money was just flowing like water. One day my attorney asked me to come to his office to go over the evidence the feds had against me. When I took a look at the stack of paperwork and email recorded files and text chains between myself and the clients, I dealt with I said to myself I'm going to jail for sure.

My attorney had to have had at least 2 to 3 ft. high of paperwork and discovery that would be used against me in court. I'm like dam I will never be able to get out of this one.

About a week later the Federal Agents called me in for an interview to discuss my background history as this would be used to determine how much time if any I would get from the judge. As I began to talk with them, I had to relive the moment of being placed in foster care, moving out of the house several times, and getting arrested on several occasions for driving and riding in stolen cars. Looking at the situation at the time my life was f*cked up from the age of 15 all the way up to when I got caught by the Feds in 2009. I only masked my pain by making money and trying to live a glamorous life knowing that what I was doing was wrong. Looking at the charges I was faced with Interstate Transportation of Stolen goods would result in me facing about 37 -40 months. In the federal court, your time isn't calculated based on years but rather in months.

For the whole remainder of 2009, I walked on eggshells wondering what the outcome of my court case would be. I continued on, living my daily life and working two part-time jobs to help support my family one of which was a job working for a publishing company that delivered the daily news. The job was cool, but you had to wake up very early in the morning around 3:00 a.m. to get the job completed, as most of the deliveries had to be completed by 6:00 a.m. My customers were good to me and although I didn't see them often, they always tipped me pretty well, and the Christmas of 2009 they sent me $10,000 in total between all my customers.

Fall of 2010 around October, I went back to Federal Court and was there to plead guilty or not guilty to the charges. The judge looked at me and said, Mr. Jones how do you plea to the charges my reply was "guilty". He looked at me and said are you sure I said "yes". By this time, I had been doing a lot of research on how Federal Courts operate and found that they have a 99.9% conviction rate due to most of the time people telling on one another. Between that and the discovery against me I was sold on my decision to plead guilty.

After pleading guilty the judge told me that he would schedule a date in April of 2011 to come back for sentencing. So, between October 2010 leading up to April 2011, I had absolutely no clue what was going to happen when I went back to court all I knew was something was going to happen and I just didn't know what. April came around and I had to deliver a statement of remorse for my actions and had to make sure that it was as truthful and honest as possible. The judges who are appointed in these cases know when they are dealing with a bullshi*ter.

Unfortunately for me, I was dealing with the toughest just in the Courthouse, so I knew for sure I'd be doing at minimum 3 years. After reviewing some of the documents in front of him and put his head up and pulled his glasses down from his face. He said to me Mr. Jones you appear to be a nice family man and have possessed a strong work ethic, but you must pay for your actions.

At that moment I took a large gulp because of everything he said prior to paying for my actions. The judge looked up at me and said I will now sentence you now. I could feel the sweat pouring down my forehead, my wife was there in the courtroom sitting behind me. Moments passed and then the judge said I am sentencing you to 1 year and a day. During my research on the sentencing guidelines, I knew by the judge giving me 1 day that my time would be reduced by 60 days which ultimately would make me only have to do 10 months. Up until this point, I had already been waiting just about 2 years for this day to come. In my mind I'm like 10 months I can do that in my sleep, but having a family wife and kids this would seem like an eternity for them. I was then told that my time would have to be done in Pennsylvania because there were no Federal Prisons located in Massachusetts. I'm like it is what it is as always, I knew how to face many situations, so I knew this was just other hurdle I had to get over.

The judge told me that I had to report to Allenwood, PA. on May 25 th which was about a month and a half since the day of sentencing. I mut say he was generous in letting me go home and get my affairs in order and spend some time with my family prior to having to leave. Leading up to this day I had no clue what to expect or even how the facility would look or anything. On May 25th I hopped on a plane and made my way down to PA to begin my sentence. Once I landed in PA I walked over to the bar before hopping in the cab I needed a drink bad. The bartender walked over and said where are you headed and where is your luggage I said to her "where I am going you don't need luggage" Her reply "what do you mean" I am heading to Federal Prison and won't be needing a change of clothes until close to a year. After I made that comment she held my hands and said a prayer for me which really was out of the normal and folks sitting next to me could hear her

The Scars That Healed

praying for me and once she was done they all said AMEN. The bartender said the drink is on me don't worry about paying I said, "thank you so much and thanks for the prayer".

I walked out of the airport and grabbed a cab. The driver said where are you headed sir my reply "MCI Allenwood" After I said that the cab driver had an ill stare on his face as if he wanted me to get out of the cab. He then asked for the cab fare up front before driving off. Being in his position and seeing where I was headed, I could understand why he felt the way he did, so I didn't take it personal. As we drove closer to the institute, I could see the huge fences surrounded the compound which housed over 1500 inmates. There were so many guys out in the yard some just walking the yard, some playing basketball and others working out. It was time for me to face reality knowing that the next 10 months I will be right here with these guys. I walked in the facility up to the front desk and the Correction Officers looked at me and said are you here for an interview?

My reply "no I am here to check in" they looked at me and said a guy your size we could surely us on our team. I'm like dam here these guys are thinking that I was here for a job but ultimately there to begin serving my time. I thought to myself if something were to happen to me my parents would never know. Me and mom got into a big blowout prior to me leaving so at the time weren't even speaking and I was too ashamed to tell my dad. The only people that knew where I was, was my sister Angela and my wife, kids, and her immediate family. Before I knew it the male officers began the process and had me take off all of my belongings and place them in a box to be shipped back to my home. Moments later a female C.O. came up to get me and told me to change into some kakis and put on these boots that were so hard on my feet and gave me some bed linen.

Once I changed, she began to lead me to my unit and asked how much time did I have? When I told her 10 months, she said you'll be going home before you know it. She said just stay busy and don't get wrapped up in the riff raff and you'll be fine. When I got down to the unit a bunch of dudes walked up to me and was like "oh you're from Boston? I replied yes. I was wondering how they knew where I as from it was the numbers ending 038 that signified where I came from. I ended up meeting a couple of dudes in my unit one named Zo and a cool ass dude named Rick from Intervale. Here I was trying to get acclimated to this new setting and hoping that all goes well for me here. We didn't have a door or bars on our rooms it was basically like going to college with a huge fence around it. I met a few other guys one named David who was serving 20 years for a drug charge and another guy they called Wiseman. Wiseman was like a mentor to me behind the wall and would always get on me for being a jokester and told me I needed to start taking things serious and stop clowning around.

I had to remind myself that although this was a minimum secured facility the problems can pop off at any time. Many of the guys there were from Baltimore and they rolled thick through the yard. If you were to get into a beef with them, you were looking at fighting at least 50 guys or maybe more because it wasn't just one coming, they are coming with a force. I ended up getting really cool with many of them one dude they called Bluff one named Reagan and a dude named Moe who was like the cats from B'mores God.

While there I started taking many classes and working out just to keep myself busy and worked the kitchen in the early a.m. I used to find someone to walk the yard with and I'd walk the track for hours and make myself tired enough to have a good night's rest. I joined the flag football team also to get some extra recreation. The time just seemed to fly buy and before I knew it, it was time for me to leave. In January of 2012, I was transferred to a halfway house in Boston to finish up my last 90 days which was cool. Wiseman came to my room around 5:00 a.m. and said a prayer for me and wished me the best. During time I was away I didn't get any visits which really didn't bother me at all because I didn't want anyone to see me like that. I felt like at the time the best thing for me to do was ride the situation out continue to keep my head up and think of a plan to get back on my feet.

Once I got to the halfway house, I was so happy knowing that I could now see my wife and kids and try to regain some sort of order to my life. After I got settled in my wife brought my daughter up to see me and boy was that little girl happy to see her dad. At this time my daughter was about 8 years old and when I left I didn't have the heart to wake her up to tell her I was leaving I saw her sleeping peacefully in the bed so I just kissed her on the forehead and made my way to the airport.

At the time I was probably in the best shape of my life. Prior to going in I was drinking and eating out of control and my weight got up to about 297 lbs. I've always been a firm believer that you have to take a negative situation and turn it into a positive one. I ended up dropping about 50 lbs. just in that 1 year to the point where folks would walk right past me on the street and not even know it was me.

After my 3 months in the halfway house was done, I went back to my home in Quincy to try and keep my home together. Prior too me leaving me and my wife weren't on the best of terms, but we tried to make things work but unfortunately, they did not. About two months of being home we both came to the conclusion that it was not going to work, and I ended up moving out. I've never been separated from my kids so that was hard to deal with especially knowing I had just got done separating from them for 10 months. The remainder of 2012 would be filled with a bunch of challenges one being not living with my kids and two trying to find work after this ordeal that I had just dealt with.

I moved to my friend Greg's house and would often go by my kid's house to spend time with them or just go pick them up to take them out. The good thing is that they didn't live far so I could always get to them in about 20 minutes or so. Starting the job search was one thing that would have me feeling really depressed and down often. I'd take on these temporary assignments and before I knew it, they would end and then I would grab another and that would come to an end. For the moment I began to feel hopeless all over again. I felt like God was trying to tell me to take some time out and just relax for a few. I ended up divorcing my kid's mother and started day a woman named Liz on September 8th 2012. Our first date I pulled up at her house she came out with a black dress on and walked down the driveway with a stride that was filled with grace.

We ended up having dinner at the Inn at Bay Pointe in Quincy. While on the date I really didn't have much money due to my work situation, so I took the bottle filled with change out of my room and returned it for the actual cash. I knew at some point I would have to tell Liz about my whole situation but wanted to do it when the timing was right. A few months after we dated in November 2012, I ended up driving down to North Carolina to visit my father. I called him on the phone, and he was so happy to hear from me. He said son where have you been? I have been so worried about you I had the Quincy Police looking for you and had no clue where you were. I replied back saying "dad I will explain another time. I went on to say where are you he said I am at Harris Teeter which was located right next to his complex. My dad didn't even know I was already in his town of Greensboro, North Carolina. So, I walked in the store and my father was bending over to pick up some last items from the grocery store for Thanksgiving. I crept up behind him and said "Sir can you tell me where the coffee is located? My dad stood up with a smile from ear to ear and hugged me tight. It took everything in me not to drop a tear from my eye because I left my father and mother for over a year not knowing where I was.

I showed up at my uncle Dewayne's house for Thanksgiving and I must say it was the best Thanksgiving ever. All of my aunts, cousins and uncles where there and it felt so good to see them all. It's funny how God has a way of bringing things together for the greater good. My last night in North Carolina I stayed at my father's house with both her and my stepmom. I woke up at about 6:00 a.m. and started getting my belongings together to hit the road. My father walked me to the door and began to start crying and kept saying I love you son at that point I had water flowing from my eyes.

The last thing my father said to me before I left out of his house was "son I thought you didn't want to be bothered with me anymore" I replied back why would you think that he said " I haven't heard from you in over a year and you never kept in contact with me and we were talking every week leading up to a year ago. Feeling bad I still was not ready to tell my father what happened, but I promised him that I would soon, but I would do it over the phone. I gave both my father and stepmom a hug and kiss goodbye and I made my way to Route 40, to 85 North to head back to Boston.

This road trip did me some good because it gave me a lot of time to think about my life and which direction it was heading. I knew for sure that the pathway to rebuilding would not be an easy one. The way life felt at the moment it appeared as though all of the steps on the ladder were breaking when

I stepped on them to reach a higher plateau. While driving my girlfriend Liz kept checking in on me to make sure that I was safe on the road. We talked periodically my whole time driving and at the time she was worried because she thought I had moved to North Carolina after meeting her. At the time Liz didn't know what I had just gone through, but I was going to tell her one day when the timing was right.

My dad ended up calling me when I got right around Maryland and said son I need to know where you were. I said dad I was in Federal Prison after that comment he said Eric why didn't you tell me. Honestly dad I felt very ashamed and didn't know how you would take this news. Looking at everything I had been through leading up to this point my father felt like I had just written him off since we hadn't talked. He said to me did your mom know where you were at? I said no. Did your sister Angela know where you were? I said yes.

One of the greatest things about both me and my sister's bond was that she loved me whether I was right, wrong, or indifferent. The level of love she showed me from the time of being a little kid entering adulthood was amazing. I continued making my way up 85 North to 95 North traveling steadily to Boston. The ride lasted a little under 12 hours, but it was much needed coming off the recent venture in my life.

In December I applied for a job working as a Customer Service Representative (temporary) for a dental insurance company. The job was fast-paced and came with quite a bit of responsibility helping dentists and members with issues etc. After about 5 months I worked my way up to becoming permanent and received the Rising Star award for being one of the best Customer Service Representatives. Throughout all of 2013, I remained taking phone calls and finally started to feel like things were falling back in place for me which was a great feeling. At the beginning of 2014, I was approached by the Workforce Director to join her team as a Workforce Coordinator, and jumped at the opportunity.

This job gave me the opportunity to now be off the phones but in charge of managing the phone lines to make sure the call center was meeting their A.S.A. Average Speed of Answer. In the Fall of 2014 around September, I applied to Curry College to give it another go. To my surprise, this time around I was accepted and began working on my Bachelor s Degree in Business. Going back to school at this time kind of made me feel nervous, especially knowing that most of the class was much younger than I. At the time of enrollment, I was about 42 years old, working full-time and trying to figure out the best way to balance things out in life. As the courses moved along, I became comfortable with the workload and after taking Accounting 1 and 2 in the Fall semester I received an A in both classes.

Since I was excelling both at work and in school I felt as though it was time to let my girlfriend know everything that I had been through prior to meeting her. Not knowing how she would feel about what I was going to say was the part that made me the most nervous, but it had to be done. We ended up meeting at a small restaurant to have dinner and afterward, we went to the car and talk. My exact words to her were "Liz prior to meeting you I had to do some time in Federal Prison" and if you feel as though you can't carry on with our relationship I understand I would just rather you hear it from me versus someone else. I think at the time Liz looked at my overall demeanor as a man and how much I cared for my kids and the work ethic she looked at me and said "Eric we are fine" Phewwww

In December 2014, we had a Christmas Party at my girlfriend's house titled Jingle Jam which was held in her basement. Many of our family and friends attended and we all enjoyed the evening listening to music, drinking and eating. Little did my girlfriend know that I was going to propose to her before the night was up and only a few people know of this. The night was moving right along and then I built up the courage to ask her. I asked everyone to come to the basement and then I grabbed the microphone walked over to her opened the ring box and asked her to marry me and she said yes.

 I knew at that moment things in life were going to turn around for the best and I was ready for all life had to offer. At the time this was my second marriage and, also hers, so we knew what we wanted from one another. Our guests all hugged and kissed us and we started passing around shots and drinking wine and beer in celebration of our engagement. Liz grabbed both of her sons and began to cry. I knew that she struggled quite often prior to our meeting but for one I felt like I was in the right place at the right time versus the wrong one.

 In June of 2015, I received another promotion at my job as an Account Coordinator, and prior to that purchased a 2007 Chrysler 300. It seemed as though, the wheels of life just kept moving along and things were staying on track. On August 22nd of 2015, I and Liz got married and had a destination wedding in St. Petersburg, Florida the only attendees from our family who witnessed the ceremony were her two aunts and soon after my aunt in-laws. The weather was great, and we had a coordinator plan everything out for us before I knew it I was heading to the beach in my powder blue suit jacket, bowtie, and white linen pants. Liz was accompanied to the beach by her aunts and we both were directed onto the beach to meet the officiant. We both wrote vows to one another and soon after were pronounced husband and wife.

 After we returned back home to Massachusetts, we ended up having a celebration of love event and invited all of hers from Brockton and mine from Boston. The night went so well, and both of our families had the opportunity to meet one another. Both of my brothers flew up from North Carolina with their wives and my dad and stepmother. One of the greatest moments of it all was being in the same place will all of my siblings and my dad being able to witness it also. I moved out to Brockton after getting married and continued on working my position as an account coordinator. I felt like for once that this dark cloud finally went away, and I wouldn't have to worry about trouble coming my way, and accepted this new chapter in my life as a refresher.

In February 2016 and the other employees were released from work early because of the heavy snow. On my way home I was hungry, so I stopped off at Simco's on the Bridge to grab a hot dog and after I left, I ended up getting stuck in the snow. My car at the time was rear-wheel drive so it made it hard to maneuver in such stormy conditions. Before I knew it I heard a loud pop come from my engine and a light smoke come from underneath the hood. All of a sudden, I hopped out of the car not knowing what would happen next.

The front end of my vehicle instantly went up in flames and the smoke increased and kept getting higher and higher. I was standing close to my car but a distance away from it my clothes smelled like smoke and all I could remember was looking up into the sky and thanking God for giving me the ability to act quickly had I not done so I wouldn't be here. Due to the fire, the car was deemed a total loss, but luckily enough I had a rental car as part of my vehicle insurance package. About 2 months later I ended up buying a 2015 Nissan Altima and shortly after two months of the purchase I was rear-ended by a Boston Firefighter who was driving drunk. The

first thing I thought to myself is here comes that dark cloud again. I was stopped at a light on Gallivan Blvd. and before you know it BANG my car was struck so hard from behind that it ended up causing about $13,000 in damages. I was so mad that evening and kept thinking how could, someone, cause this much damage? and I was just sitting still not moving.

Before I knew it, the Boston Police and State Troopers showed up on the scene and the person who hit my vehicle fled the scene and could not be found. After a search of a few minutes, they were able to apprehend the person who was driving drunk. This situation took a totally different spin in my life I had to stop taking classes due to back and neck injuries and ultimately had to place my schooling on hold for a while. Here I was still working, out of school and a new vehicle that I had just purchased was damaged. Throughout the rest of 2016, I dealt with a lot of pain

from the accident and was lucky to get 3-4 hours of sleep every night. The days just seemed to get longer and longer, and the pain seemed to be unbearable.

In early 2017, I went down to North Carolina to visit with my family but especially went to check on my uncle Robert because he was in the hospital at the time. It felt weird to me to see my uncle in a hospital bed because he was always so vibrant and full of life and made everyone laugh.

Things with him seemed to be going well and I prayed that all would be well with him. After visiting with him I spent a couple of days in North Carolina just catching up with family and then prepared to make my way back home. As soon as I got back to Boston the day after returning home my father called to inform me that my Uncle Robert had passed away. I dropped the phone in disbelief, and I could hear my father saying my name "Eric, Eric, Eric". At the time I was at a loss for words and really did not know what to say. All I kept thinking about were all of the good times I shared with him and how protective he was over his kids, nieces, and nephews.

It was time to prepare for funeral services for my uncle and I knew that it would not be easy for me. Uncle Robert was more than just an uncle, he was like a father figure and big brother to me, and, losing that was something I was not quite sure I would get over. At the funeral, I cried so hard knowing how much I was going to miss him. A few days later I made my way back home and the entire ride back to Boston all I kept thinking about was my uncle knowing that I would not be able to speak to him again.

Once I got back home my sister Angela was diagnosed with congested heart failure. It seemed like that dark cloud had returned, back to my life, and always seemed like there was no way to escape it. Praying for the best for my sister stayed heavy on my mind at the time I wasn't ready for any more bad news. Every opportunity I got, I went to Boston Medical Center to see her and Angela was telling me that she was feeling much better so I knew she was in good mental space and she would fight through this. The doctors had prescribed some medication for her to take and also some other health tips. Finally, it was time for her to come home and I was so happy and drove there to pick her up and bring her home. We talked along the way and my sister spoke about changes she was going to make in regard to her dieting.

In 2018 my sister ended up going back to the hospital due to her congested heart failure. This time around she stayed in the hospital for quite a few days as the doctors monitor her health closely pertaining to her heart condition. As before I always made it up to the hospital to check on her to make sure she was okay and assist her in any way possible. The relationship that I and my sister shared for many years always helped to keep us drawn close to one another and the bond could never be broken. After about a week or so my sister was released from the hospital and was able to go home. This time around she was placed on oxygen which she had to intake periodically throughout the day.

Just as any other day I would check in on my sister to make sure that she was sticking to the prescribed plan that the doctor's and nurses put in place for her. My sister would always tell me that she was sticking to the plan to avoid going back into the hospital. As time went on, I could see that she was taking her condition serious and did her best to maintain a healthier lifestyle.

In 2019, I returned, back to Curry College to continue pursuing my degree in Business. At the time I had been out of school for more than 3 years due to my car accident. I knew at this time I would have to push through even harder to get my goals achieved from an academic standpoint. In speaking to my education advisor, I started doubling up on some courses by enrolling in Massasoit Community College while still attending Curry College. Early 2020 Covid-19 swept through the country and placed many things on hold and caused many things like school and work to become remote settings.

Around April of 2020 my sister went back into the hospital as she was dealing with complications breathing. This had to be the toughest situation for me to deal with at the time as I could not go to the hospital to see her because of the pandemic. The only communication we had during that time was through Facetime on our Iphones.

With my sister in the hospital, it worried me a lot because I didn't know if she would be exposed to Covid while being there to treat her heart condition. Trying to focus on school and also work was an ultimate challenge for me at this point, but I knew that with all I had endured in the past that this would be another situation in which I would have to dig deep and find the inner strength and rely on my faith in God to cover my sister while she is in the hospital. Around the first week of June my sister had been moved to a rehabilitation center in Stoughton, MA. Things were really starting to look up and I knew for sure that my sister was on the road to recovery. She would call me often around 7:00 a.m. and we would face time and it felt good to see her face seeing that most of her time spent in the hospital she was hooked up to machines. That itself bothered me not knowing what the next day would bring.

About a week later I was laying down in the bed on a Sunday afternoon and received a call from my friend Keith. As always, we greeted each other and asked how the other one was doing.

Shortly after he said Eric, I think something happened to one of your family members, but I am not sure exactly what. My friend Keith told me that his mom said that something happened to a family member of mine in North Carolina. I know that his mother only knew of my family members in North Carolina my aunt Varnetta, Uncle Dewayne, and my cousin Aaron. At the time I didn't know which of these three were harmed and/or how serious it was.

Moments after I received a phone call saying that my cousin Aaron had drowned and at that moment the rest of my day was filled with worrisome thoughts. Each day after that while trying to focus on work I would log on to the local news in North Carolina to see if any progress had been made to find my cousin. Out of all of my cousins, Aaron was the youngest on my father's side and always the first person I would see when I traveled to North Carolina and drove in to Greensboro.

For several days my family would be up at Lake Norman looking for my cousin along with his girlfriend. My prayers all week went into overdrive because I needed my cousin to be found and I knew at the time how I felt so I could only imagine the hurt and pain his parents were dealing with.

The following weekend one of my cousins called me and told me that they found my cousin Aaron and he had passed. Immediately the day after on Father's Day in 2020 I flew out of Boston to Charlotte to show my support for my family. The whole plane ride I thought heavily to myself about what words of encouragement can I offer to my aunt and uncle who just lost their son. The only thing I could think of was just hugging them both when I saw them, telling them that I love them.

As the week went on my family prepared to say their final goodbye to my cousin Aaron. I thought to myself that the cycle of life has been different lately as many parents are burying their children as it should be the other way around but I had to rely on the statement "God makes no mistakes" in order to pull through. I wasn't able to stay for the actual funeral but did attend the viewing and it hurt me so bad inside to fathom the thought of not being able to talk to my cousin Aaron again. He was only 28 at the time very vibrant and full of life and cared for so many people and had a huge impact on those he met and the ones he didn't through his podcast.

It was time to fly back home and the whole time I was staying in constant contact with my sister checking on her well-being to make sure that she was okay. Upon my return, my sister told me that she was informed that she would be leaving the facility on July 6. I was so happy to hear the news and thanked the man above for keeping her not only in good health but in good spirits also. The day had finally come when my sister was able to leave the rehabilitation center and I knew that this day going forward I would have to look after her to make sure that she was doing everything needed to keep her in good health.

The same day she came home she was taken back to the hospital that same night. I had no clue which hospital she was in at the time and stayed up all night calling every hospital in

Boston trying to locate her. The first call I made was to Boston Medical Center seeing that she was always treated there, but after calling she was not there from what they told me. Staying up all night in a panic I was not able to find out where my sister was which made it very hard to even get a minute of sleep.

The next morning my sister called me via facetime on her phone and she looked really tired like she hadn't slept a wink. I said to her Angela where are you she replied, "Boston Medical Center". After she said that I told her that I tried calling there looking for her, but they said she wasn't there. I think it was a timing issue due to the time I called they hadn't checked her in yet. Looking at my sister's face her eyes were swollen and looked as if she needed to get some much- needed rest. Soon after the nurse came in and told my sister it was time to take her medication. I told my sister to get some rest and that I would talk to her later. Seeing how tired my sister looked I just carried on with my workday and let her have some time to catch up on her sleep if needed.

I was able to get a good night's rest knowing where my sister was and knew that she was at least in good hands with the nurses and doctors. The morning after on July 8 I woke up refreshed and made myself a cup of coffee as I normally do prior to logging on to work. My sister didn't call me at 7:00 like she usually did the days and months before. At the time I really didn't think anything of it and just continued on with my day. Looking at the clock the time continued to pass 7:00 o'clock turned to 8 o'clock and so on. Around 12:00 one of my friends called me on the phone and asked if I wanted to come by for a little gathering at the pool.

Something in my gut told me that things weren't right, but I didn't think anything of it and told my friend I have to make sure that my sister was okay before I make a move. As I continued to work, I looked at the clock and it was 2:00 p.m.

I really started to worry at this point because that wasn't like my sister to not call at least by that time. In a panic, I started making phone calls to people with who my sister was closest with that I had contact numbers for. The first call made was to her friend Barbara the phone rang a few times and Barbara picked up. I asked, "Barbara have you heard from Angela"? she replied back no. I hung up the phone and called my sister's phone a few times over and she didn't pick up.

About an hour or so later Barbara called back and said that another friend of her and my sisters had called her to tell her that my sister passed. In hearing this I was on my deck drinking a bottle of beer I smashed the glass bottle and began to scream as my ears could not believe what I was hearing. I asked Barbara where my sister was, and she told me she was in Cambridge. At the time I couldn't think of anyone my sister knew who lived in Cambridge but didn't really question it because I and my sister have many mutual friends and some not. After getting the address to the location where my sister was my wife drove me to Cambridge. The whole time in the car I kept saying to myself this has to be a mistake or some kind of hoax. My sister at the time was only 50 and I just couldn't imagine her leaving me.

After we pulled up to the address in Cambridge an officer walked over to me and said is your name, Eric? I replied back "yes," he said I am so sorry for your loss. At that moment I felt like all of the air in my lungs had just escaped my body and I stood there lifeless. The officer said I'm going to grab a bag with your sister's belongings and will be right back to you. During this time, me and my mom hadn't talked for about 5 years for different reasons.

I called my father on the phone and after giving him the news he son I'm going to have to call you back. It really hurt me, even more, to hear my dad crying on the phone. My mind was steadily racing, and I paced back and forth on the sidewalk waiting for the officer to bring my sister's belongings to me. I stood there in disbelief because although I knew it was a reality, I still refused to believe it. After all, I and my sister have been through together I really did not want our chapter to end this way.

Moments after calling my dad he called me back and said your mother wants you to call her. In my mind I'm asking myself the question how will this conversation go? In the past, it ultimately ended up with arguments between her and me, so I had to brace myself for the conversation. I called my mom on the phone and she answered and said Eric your sister passed away? I replied back "yes mom Angie is no longer with us in the physical". My mom then asked where are you going to have your sister's body transported? I told her about J.B. Johnson's funeral home. I never thought I would see the day when I and my sister would part ways. We parted ways as teenagers and now she is no longer here with me and I knew the days ahead would be an uphill battle.

The following week I took time off to get things prepared for my sister's funeral regarding everything from picking out a casket to flowers etc. By the time the day of the funeral came, I was so exhausted from sleeping literally 2-3 hours a night that week. I must have drank, alcohol and smoked weed until my body felt numb and then took a nice hot shower and repeated the days after. At my sister's funeral, I broke down and cried so hard my suit jacket was drenched with tears I could not believe that it was over.

In the following weeks ahead, I tried my best to stay focused between school and work and just try to maintain everyday living. I continued on taking my courses in school and kept pushing along. Despite the fact that my head was filled with thoughts of my cousin Aaron and my sister Angela I knew

I needed to push through some things as they would have wanted me to.

My sister was always my protector and my mom would tell me that often which is why it made it even harder after her death. The following Summer in 2021 I would sit on the deck and smoke a cigar and one day I and my wife heard a bird chirping right over the house. We both listened close and the bird was actually chirping my name "Eric, Eric, Eric, Eric". In disbelief, I recorded it and let my mom hear it. Once my mom heard the recording she said when you and Angela were little, she would always say your name just like that to get you to stop crying. I was in awe by my mother's comment and figured this was my sister's way of letting me know she was ok.

Hearing this bird chirping and saying my name actually soothed my soul somewhat and started to place me in good spirits. As the year progressed, I started getting closer to my 50th birthday and often reflected back on how my sister lost her life at the same age. Leading up to my birthday I knew for sure I would miss my sister calling me on the phone and saying, "Happy

Birthday Fella". I had a huge red and black 50th event and strangely enough without knowing my decorator knew my sister very well. When I told her who my sister was, she began to cry and said Angela has been around my family for years. I knew that it was the man above who sent her my way to make sure my party decorations looked great.

At my party I gave a small speech and referenced my sister. Having my childhood friends and family around me to celebrate a milestone was one of the best feelings ever. I had a few photos of me and my sister to show her presence in a spiritual way. January 2022 began, and this was the year I had been waiting for, for quite some time especially starting school in 2014 and then having to take a break in 2016 after my car accident. Coming off of a 3 yr. hiatus was something I thought about when I started classes back up in 2019. Trying my best to complete my course work in time for graduation 2022 was something I was determined to get completed.

Thinking back to my teenage years when I first applied to Curry College and being denied proved to me that all things could be done on my time and no one else's. One of the hardest pills to swallow back then was being denied access to the school. Although I knew I wasn't ready for college life it still bothered me to not be accepted. Through my hard work and dedication and pushing through all of the obstacles that life threw my way in 50 years I knew at this moment in life it was my time to shine. May 2022 came around and it was graduation day at the Xfinity Center in Mansfield, MA. The day had my stomach filled with butterflies knowing that this moment was finally going to happen.

Standing in line an getting registered for the day I thought something may go wrong but the tides had finally turned, and I was well on my way to get through the events of the day. We marched into the big stadium and took our seats according to the program we were enrolled in. The moment had come it was time to announce all of the students who were graduating from the Bachelor of Arts Degree program. Finally, they called my name "Eric Jones" I could hear my wife, daughter and friends screaming my name as I walked to receive my certificate of participation in the Curry College 2022 Commencement.

Looking at myself on the big screen at Xfinity Center was a moment where I had to take a deep breath and realize that God did all the things in my life on his time and not my own. A few weeks later I received my actual degree in the mail and ordered a frame to put it in. The same week a few days later I received a letter from Curry College informing me that I achieved made it to the Dean's List for the Spring Semester.

Throughout all of the pain and suffering, I endured in life the twist and turns are what molded me into the person I am today. It's not about what you go through. it's about how hard you are willing to fight through the obstacles of life. We all have a life plan which is designed for us at birth some of it includes good things and some bad. The hardest determining factor is to know when things will take place in your life. They often say that if you stay ready, you don't have to worry about getting ready. Looking back on my own life experience it was a roller coaster ride that seemed to be never-ending. I strongly believe the strongest soldiers in life are aligned to fight through the toughest of battles. Fighting through all of life's obstacles was the best experience I could ask for.

Each day I woke up and opened my eyes I knew the day would come when the scars of life would finally heal.

AMPLIFLUENCE
AMPLIFY YOUR INFLUENCE

You're the Expert, but are you struggling to Monetize your Authority?

Amplify Your Influence in 3 Sessions

Speak Your Message **Publish Your Message** **Convert Your Message**

Authors and Speakers often find themselves struggling to build a strategy that actually makes them money.

Check Out All Of Our 'Live' Tour Stops

amplifluence.com

SCAN FOR TOUR INFO

More Books From Perfect Publishing

www.PerfectPublishing.com

More Books From **Perfect Publishing**

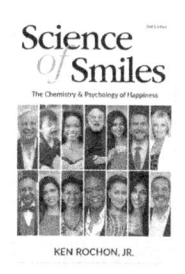

www.PerfectPublishing.com

Made in the USA
Middletown, DE
17 November 2022